Anna Kruger studied Astrology at the Faculty of
Astrological Studies and at the Centre for Psychological
Astrology under Liz Greene, one of the most successful
astrologers of recent years. Anna has been a practising
astrologer since 1982.

To my parents.

ASTROLOGY DESIGNS FOR LIVING

ANNA KRUGER

ILLUSTRATIONS BY JANE RAY

An OPTIMA book

© Anna Kruger 1989

First published in 1989 by
Macdonald Optima, a division of
Macdonald & Co. (Publishers) Ltd

A Member of Maxwell Pergamon Publishing Corporation Plc

British Library Cataloguing in Publication Data
Kruger, Anna.
   Astrology: designs for living.
   1. Astrology. Psychological aspects
   I. Title
   133.5'01'9

   ISBN 0-356-15516-1

Macdonald & Co. (Publishers) Ltd
66-73 Shoe Lane
London EC4P 4AB

Typeset in Century Schoolbook by
Leaper & Gard Ltd, Bristol, England

Printed and bound in Great Britain by
The Guernsey Press Co. Ltd,
Guernsey, Channel Islands

THANKS

To Rodney Wilson for months of support, Harriet Griffey and Ean Begg for encouragement, Lawrence Webb, Robin Hayfield and Theresa Jacobs for helpful comments, Odyssey Bookshop for resources, and clients and friends for sharing their charts.

To expect the unexpected shows a thoroughly modern intellect.

Oscar Wilde

CONTENTS

1.
EXPLODING A FEW MYTHS

Astrology first began to interest me when I discovered that there seemed to be some kind of pattern to my friendships and relationships. Looking into the field of astrology further, I found I could relate this pattern to astrology's larger design. Here was a system which, to me, made some sense of my experience and answered some of the questions in my mind, such as why did I keep having relationships with either Aquarian or Sagittarian men, and why was I drawn to Cancers but often felt uneasy with them? Eventually a friend drew up my birth chart and I discovered that astrology was a far more sophisticated art than I had previously imagined. What really fascinated me was the discovery that my birth chart, with its intricate pattern of signs and planets, confirmed the existence of different facets of my personality, some of which I had always been vaguely aware. Not all of these, I might add, were flattering!

At that point I decided to have a chart reading done by

a well-known astrologer and then went on to spend three years studying the subject, reading in my spare time as many books as I could both on astrology and psychology. These two disciplines complement each other, since both are concerned with what motivates us to act as we do and what influences our choices. By taking a psychological approach to astrology it is possible to perceive how we all weave our life's pattern according to our own design. I began to see how easy it had been to blame others for the flaws in my own particular piece of fabric, as well as why I had problems with Cancers!

The real significance of astrology lies in its value as a tool for *living*. The insights it offers into our characters enables us to perceive the underlying meaning to the patterns in our lives. It enables us to become aware of the various cycles, and in particular the tendency of things to come back again. A knowledge of astrology helps us to identify and acknowledge those patterns. With awareness comes the possibility for change, so we are less likely to repeat our mistakes unconsciously. Serious astrology recognises that none of us are as simplistic or one-dimensional as the popular, uninformed view would have us believe. It treats us with the respect I think we deserve.

POPULAR MISCONCEPTIONS

Misconceptions about astrology abound. Many people hold an opinion on the validity of astrology, but few speak from an informed point of view. The widespread misconceptions about astrology made me think of a particular story I once read. One day a professor visited the house of a Japanese Zen master to find out more about the teachings of Zen Buddhism. The master set down an empty cup before his guest and proceeded to pour tea into it. He continued to pour long after the cup was full and the tea spilled over the edges and on to the table. Finally the professor could restrain himself no longer and begged the Zen master to stop pouring. The master explained that the professor was like an overflowing cup, full of his own opinions and preconceptions. In order to learn about Zen, he said, it was necessary to first empty one's cup. The same applies to astrology.

Let me begin by looking at a few of the more widespread assumptions so that we can begin to empty the cup.

Sun Sign Columns

If you thought astrology was all about reading your star sign column in the newspaper or in your monthly magazine, then think again! This would be rather like assuming that all there is to cooking is following the instructions on the packet. Similarly with a photograph, the facial expression captures only one particular mood, it does not reveal every facet of our character. Nor does what you read in your Sun sign column tell you all there is to know about yourself, let alone present an accurate picture of what astrology is all about. After all, there is a limit to how many tall dark strangers you can meet in one year!

When you read that you 'are a Virgo' that simply means that on the day you were born the Sun, seen from the earth, was travelling through that section of the sky which belongs to the constellation of Virgo. The Sun spends roughly a month in Virgo, and in each of the eleven other signs of the zodiac, entering a fresh sign on or about the 21st. The Sun moves very slowly during the course of a day, but the view of the heavenly pattern from earth changes hour by hour.

Other factors which go to make up a chart alter the design much more quickly. The Ascendant, a very important point, can change degree in as little as four minutes (unless you were born near the equator or the north or south pole). It determines where the divisions between the 'houses' of your individual chart will fall. This means that someone born two minutes later than you, in the same place, could have a different rising sign. If you were born when the very last degree of, for example, Pisces, was rising over the eastern horizon, your friend born two minutes later could have Aries rising. Sun sign

columns do not take into account either the fast-moving
Ascendant or the Moon which spends only two and a
half days in each sign. So an awful lot of people born
when the Sun was in Virgo will have not only their
Ascendant, but also their Moon in different signs. The
Sun, Moon and Ascendant are the three most important
factors in the birth chart, but Sun sign columns are not
sufficiently sophisticated to take everyone's individual
combination of signs into account. They assume, of
necessity, that your Sun sign is the same as your rising
sign or Ascendant, although for most people this is not the
case. Then, there are the positions of the other eight
planets to calculate and integrate into the circle of the
horoscope. So there are, besides the Sun, many other
component parts of an individual birth chart, all of which
significantly alter and enrich the design.

There will be more about the nuts and bolts of the
horoscope later. What I hope is becoming apparent now is
that the Sun sign columns at best can only give a vague,
very general indication of what is in store for Ms Virgo on
a particular day. What is more, there is no such person as
Ms Average Virgo, that's rather like saying there is a Mr
and Mrs Average American, or that if you want a reaction
to your policy on defence or a new brand of toothpaste you
should seek the advice of that well-known figure, the 'Man
in the Street'. No such average people exist, except
perhaps in the minds of politicians and marketing
executives. Just as we all have a unique set of fingerprints,
so we all have a unique horoscope which contains 10
planets, in particular positions, forming particular
patterns and engaging in a particular dialogue within us.
This means that we do not fit easily into the 12
homogenous Sun sign categories, like so many pigeons in
their holes!

Sun sign columns are neither particularly useful nor
particularly useless. They are fun to read on the journey to
or from work, or to liven up the coffee break. Taken with a
pinch of salt, they satisfy that urge in all of us to know
what's round the next corner or what the weekend has in

store — but be sure to make it a large pinch of salt. We humans are complex creatures, capable of playing many roles, even during the course of one day. Most of us could rival a theatrical production with our own personal cast of characters, including those we wouldn't even give a walk-on part. No-one is as stereotyped as those ubiquitous columns would have us believe. They are merely the tip of the astrological iceberg.

DO THE PLANETS REALLY INFLUENCE US?

The physical planets out there in space are simply focusing points. They exert a symbolic influence on our life experiences. Weird and wonderful planetary rays do not beam down on us poor, unsuspecting mortals. If they did, surely sunburn would be more than just a darkening of the skin? It is true that planetary bodies do have demonstrable physical effects, like the Moon on the tides, marine creatures, or the growing cycle of plants, to name but a few and this is a fascinating area in itself. If you want to know more about it, try reading *Supernature* by Lyall Watson.

Astrology, however, is not concerned with this aspect of planetary influence. Instead, it identifies a correlation between the different planetary energies and our lives on earth on a symbolic, not a literal, level. The planets neither make us who we are, nor cause things to happen to us – 'The stars incline; they do not compel.' Rather, between the planets, up there, and us, down here, there exists a 'synchronisation'.

Synchronicity is not an easy concept to grasp. It involves accepting the possibility that the outer world in which things happen is very closely linked with that inner world each of us privately inhabits. If you have ever experienced what is known as *déjà vu* or a series of coincidences, you have caught a glimpse of that amazing world which seems to defy the laws of space and time. To give you just one example, in his book *Dreams of Dragons*, scientist Lyall Watson recounts the true story of the evening all 15 members of the choir in a small town in Nebraska were late. They were all delayed for different reasons, from being unable to start the car to ironing a dress. However on that particular evening, the boiler blew up and the empty church was totally wrecked. Similar experiences abound – you have probably got one to recount yourself. And they make us think that something, somewhere, has an uncanny ability to organise things. It is almost as if there is an overall design or pattern to life, on a grand scale. Swiss psychologist C.G. Jung called this synchronicity, a principle which pays no heed to cause and effect or to time and space.

Meaningful coincidences can and do occur. Often when we think or speak about a particular person they ring up at that very moment. One friend used to arrive at the door, sometimes within an hour of us wondering aloud where he was and what he was up to. This was definitely uncanny since sometimes we didn't know he was living in the same country. Astrology is comfortable with this world of pattern and design with its mysterious organising principle. It is one in which the planets do not cause events – the two simply coincide. We can learn a lot about ourselves by getting in touch with this rather wonderful process of which we are a part. Anyone who has had experience of astrology at work has at least got a foot in the door.

This concept of inter-relatedness is also at the core of 'alternative' or 'complementary' medicine. Whereas orthodox medicine focuses on your disease, complementary medicine focuses on you, the person. Treatment by a practitioner of complementary medicine, for example a homeopath, involves building up a picture of your mental and emotional state, your relationship to your body and your environment, whilst noting your symptoms. Mind, emotions and body are seen as inseparable one from the other. In homeopathy we are given a minuscule dose of what produces our symptoms to mobilise our body's own healing force. We are encouraged to restore our own balance.

The interweaving of mind, emotions and body mirrors the harmonious, changing pattern of our universe. We are part of this complex design, although we don't really understand who wove it. Rather than addle our brains with such speculation, we would do better to try and sort out the tangles in our own particular bit of cloth. This is where astrology can help us, by enabling us to recognise the patterns in our own particular design.

ISN'T ASTROLOGY REALLY JUST FORTUNE TELLING?

The answer to this very common question is simple: it depends on the skill and dignity of the person reading your chart. Astrology is no more immune from charlatanism or exploitation by unscrupulous practitioners than the stock market for example. If you look hard enough among the crystal-ball brigade you are sure to find a so-called 'astrologer' who will happily serve you up a tasty dish of predictions. Certainly, many people have felt sufficiently confused, or even desperate, at some time to consult a clairvoyant, palmist, tea-leaf or card reader. I have nothing against such practitioners – they exist in response to a very real demand.

However, the approach to astrology advocated in this book is not concerned with predicting events. Attempting to foretell the future can offer no more than a temporary solution, however seriously you take it. To my mind, trying to understand what provoked the confusion which sent us hot-foot to the fortune teller in the first place is of far greater value in the long term. This is where a psychological approach to astrology can help. It can offer valuable and constructive insights into why we keep on finding ourselves in difficult situations or why we attract particular kinds of people into our lives. Of course it is much easier to visit a fortune teller – that way we can blame it all on fate. Using astrology, on the other hand, involves accepting responsibility for our actions and not everyone can face this task. Many would prefer to give someone else the responsibility of reading what lies at the bottom. But surely, given the stresses of modern living on a small overcrowded planet, it is infinitely preferable to take charge of what is definitely within our reach, namely our own lives. Astrology provides us with a map for our journey and its value lies in the opportunity of learning to read that map for ourselves.

DOES MY HOROSCOPE IMPLY THAT MY LIFE IS FATED?

> Men at some time are masters of their fates.
> The fault, dear Brutus, lies not in our stars,
> But in ourselves, that we are underlings.
> Shakespeare, *Julius Caesar*

It is perhaps this vexed question more than any other which provokes outbursts of hostility towards astrology. Certainly it is seen by those of a more orthodox religious persuasion within the Christian Church to be ample evidence of the heathen nature of astrologers. They conveniently forget that Christ's birth was heralded by a star and that it was this important celestial event which guided the Wise Men to Bethlehem. The Wise Men were almost certainly astrologers. God, it is argued, never intended that man should have either the arrogance or the temerity to consider his future as his own. Let us be very clear on this point – astrologers who work with the birth chart cannot predict specific events. They can only indicate on the basis of the horoscope that certain kinds of things, not necessarily outside events, maybe feelings or states of mind, will be around at particular times. What you choose to make of these is up to you. The astrologer can help you come to a decision which may be more appropriate for you at a particular point in your life – there is always more than one decision but certain decisions do seem more fitting than others. A skilled interpretation of your horoscope will often clarify matters for you. But your imput is crucial. In my opinion the most fruitful part of any chart reading is the dialogue between astrologer and client. Astrologers are human too – we are not oracles to be blindly obeyed, nor do many of us get much out of listening to ourselves talk or writing a long analysis of someone's chart without any feedback. We do not necessarily have the ear of the gods.

All of us are limited to the extent that we were born of particular parents, at a particular time in history, with particular characteristics of a mental, emotional, spiritual and physical nature. We cannot change our parents, travel through time, or change the aforementioned characteristics as if they were a suit of clothes. We can, however, modify our attitudes. We can learn from experience which aspects of our personalities are our strengths and which are our weaknesses. We can always try to develop the former and improve on the latter. Everyone goes through certain phases of development from birth to death. Because of the person we are, we seek out and process experiences in a certain way. The chart is a map of probabilities, modified by our family background, culture and economic circumstances. We are all fated in so far as we must start with the materials we have at hand – ourselves.

Why not make use of the insights astrology has to offer to understand better those parts of you you wish would go away? They may turn out to be areas of hidden treasure. Surely it makes more sense to work with what you've got rather than wishing you had classical good looks, a rapier wit or an IQ of 145. We may wish to justify our particular plight, whether it be physical, emotional or financial, in terms of God's will or the forces of Karma. It makes very little difference to the here and now except perhaps that such justification neatly precludes us from changing anything in our lives. Yet we still have to get on with the business of living. With the help of astrology we can begin to make some sense of the patterns we have created. Astrology enables us to connect past experiences to the present by means of studying our chart in relationship to particular planetary cycles. We can look back to a previous point in the cycle and see our present position as a chance to improve on our past situation. Our lives are our own responsibility.

CAN ASTROLOGY BE SCIENTIFICALLY PROVEN?

The first point is what constitutes scientific proof? It is my understanding that something is scientifically proven if the experiment can be replicated and the same result achieved. However, in astrology no two birth charts are exactly alike. Even identical twins are born minutes apart and in that short space of time the planetary landscape has changed. So how can we compare like with like? We can, like the *Guardian* newspaper in 1985, conduct a survey in which occupations are tested against Sun signs. But as we know, Sun signs are not the whole story and, to throw another spanner in the works, what we do for a living is not necessarily what we feel best suited to do – occupation is not necessarily vocation.

The second point is what is it exactly that should be proved? That astrology works? The proof of the pudding is, as they say, in the eating. Have a chart reading or go to classes on astrology, and see for yourself. Astrology is rather like electricity – very few of us understand the theory of electric currents, but we do know whether the light is on or off. As anyone who has been helped by astrology will tell you, it works.

Two French statisticians who set out to find out, once and for all, whether astrology really worked were pleasantly surprised by their findings. In 1984 Michel and Françoise Gauquelin published an analysis of the horoscopes of 6,000 sporting champions, 10,000 scientists, 18,000 actors, and 16,000 writers for particular character traits associated by astrologers with particular planets. In the charts of the sporting champions, Mars, planet of energy, drive, courage and will, was especially prominent. In the charts of the scientists, Saturn, the planet associated with precision, methodical behaviour, realism and control, was highlighted. In the charts of the actors,

Jupiter, the planet of expansiveness, extroversion, a certain vanity and effusiveness, was particularly dominant. Finally, in the charts of the writers, the Moon, associated with sensitivity, subtlety, imagination and creativity, was – you guessed it – strongly emphasised. More about the planets later, but as you will agree, this sort of survey, which stands up to a careful degree of scrutiny, shows that astrology can be taken seriously. As I said before, it is impossible in astrology to compare like with like, but people with particular personality traits, like those mentioned above, are attracted to those professions which give them expression. And these character traits are revealed in the horoscope.

Spurred on by the Gauquelins' findings and aided by that wonderful time-saving device, the computer, astrologers all over the world beaver away on various research projects. There is little, if any, money available for such work and the low esteem in which astrology is held makes it an unlikely field for investment. A parallel can be drawn with research into the healing properties of plants. The contraceptive pill was synthesised from the South American wild yam; the life-saving heart drug, digoxin, from the common foxglove. Things of considerable value seem to turn up in the most unlikely places. One can only speculate on the useful discoveries yet to be made in the field of astrology and applaud those who devote their spare time and limited resources to producing research reports and statistics which will satisfy even the most jaundiced critic.

WHAT IS MEANT BY 'NEW AGE' OR 'THE AGE OF AQUARIUS'?

The idea of the dawning of the New Age or Age of Aquarius was popularised by the musical *Hair* in the late 1960s and some people are puzzled as to why this new era of peace and brotherly love has not yet materialised. However, all is not as simple as the popular songs would have us believe. This 'dawning' of a New Age describes our present era which, in astrological terms, is moving through the last stages of the Age of Pisces towards the Aquarian Age. I have not yet encountered anyone who was prepared to say exactly when the Age of Aquarius begins, indeed it may have already begun. Some say that the Piscean Age began with the birth of Christ, others that it happened in AD 221. Since an Astrological Age lasts just over 2,000 years we are certainly now in a confusing period of transition between the Piscean and Aquarian Ages.

Aquarius is associated with the brotherhood of man, with new ideas, new technology, the unconventional, working in groups and yet retaining one's independence and individuality. Perhaps the 'dawning' of the Aquarian Age did begin in the late 1960s when people demonstrated in political groups for greater freedom of the individual. At the same time society began to be more ecologically aware and the wholefood movement began. Now we see the flowering of such ideas, for example, in the success of natural cleansers and cosmetics, prepared according to ecological and humanitarian principles, as well as in the increase in more 'natural', additive-free food. In the latter half of the 1980s the technological revolution began to make its presence felt in the home as well as in the workplace in the shape of the personal computer. Increased availability of information technology has given rise to the phenomenon of 'networking' – the linking of like-minded people in geographically different locations. In terms of work, many people may eventually become independent of a central office, communicating by computer from home and saving costs. The Aquarian ideal of the 'brotherhood of man' is also apparent in the concept of 'world music' which crosses language and cultural barriers to connect artists from all over the world, bringing their music before the widest possible audience.

The spirit of the Aquarian Age does seem to be abroad, but periods of transition are not without their upheavals. This in-between time can be painful and confusing since it is hard to let go of old ways of being. Old habits die hard and new ideas struggle to be born. Pluto, planet of death, rebirth and transformation entered Scorpio, in November 1983. It leaves this sign at the end of 1995 after a 12 year residence. Pluto tends to dredge up those things we prefer to keep hidden such as spy scandals, political corruption, insider dealing, child abuse, sexually transmitted diseases, and the amorous exploits of public figures – all of which have been brought out into the open and caused a certain amount of embarrassment in the last two or three years. In 1996 Uranus enters its own sign of Aquarius to be joined by Neptune two years later in 1998. Perhaps when Pluto has finished stirring up the mud in Scorpio, and Uranus and Neptune have moved into Aquarius, we will witness the awakening of a hopefully more enlightened and humanitarian Aquarian Age.

2. WHY ASTROLOGY?

WHERE DID ASTROLOGY COME FROM?

Astrology developed from our ancient ancestors' observations of the changing pattern of the skies. They needed to know when to sow and plant, as well as how to measure time or the length of a journey. Around 15,000 BC the first lunar phases were recorded and it is interesting that phrases like 'many moons ago' have survived to the present day. Such ancient civilisations sought to regulate their lives and they did so by noting the movements of the Sun, the Moon and the planets. The word 'planets' is derived from a Greek word meaning 'wanderer', but our ancestors found that far from wandering just anywhere, the planets kept to a definite path. This came to be known as the zodiac and was eventually divided into twelve parts bearing the same names as twelve of the constellations.

Such observations imply a necessity to link events on

earth with those in the sky – as above, so below, or as up there, so down here. To the ancients, the stars were a mystery, unlike the Sun or Moon which changed the temperature or the degree of light. The Sun's annual journey was connected to the seasons while its night-time disappearance became symbolic of the span of human life, moving from birth to death. Thus a religious or spiritual dimension was inherent in the observance of the movements of the 'heavenly' bodies. The main festival in the Christian Church, Christmas, is celebrated around the winter solstice. This is the time when the Sun, after reaching its lowest point in the northern hemisphere, appears to stand still, then slowly begins to climb once more. Once the shortest day is past, the light is symbolically reborn and daylight hours increase.

Around 3,000 to 2,000 BC, the ancient Mesopotamian civilisations which comprised the Babylonians, Sumerians and Assyrians, kept detailed records of the patterns in the skies and gave the Sun, Moon and the planets names of deities. It is difficult to know which came first, the planets or the gods or goddesses. Probably in such early cultures where divinities dwelt in all natural phenomena, whether in the sky or on the earth, the distinction was irrelevant. The planet and the deity were simply one and the same thing. At first the only divinity worshipped was the Goddess or Great Mother. The astrology of the Babylonians, astrologers cum astronomers *par excellence*, was centred arond Ishtar, the goddess of love. In their book *The Knot of Time*, Lindsay River and Sally Gillespie trace the roots of astrology back to the experience of wise women who observed the heavens as a whole, and the cycle of the Moon in particular. Thus women were able to determine when menstruation and pregnancy were likely to occur.

WHAT'S IN A NAME?

The names we use today for the planets are said to be
derived directly from the names of the Babylonian deities.
The Greeks matched these names to those of their own
gods and the Romans are responsible for those in current
use. Venus (Aphrodite in Greek), for example, is
equivalent to the Babylonian Ishtar, and Jupiter (Zeus in
Greek) to Marduk. We may consider such 'mythological'
names as belonging to ancient history and consign them to
the past. However, our everyday language contains many
words whose meanings derive directly from mythological
characters and, by association, from the planets. A jovial
person embodies the nature of Jupiter, cheerful and
expansive. A mercurial individual is quick-witted, like the
god Mercury, while martial, derived from Mars, describes
the fighting arts like kung fu and karate. Venus gets very
short shrift – from her we get the word venereal, the
lover's affliction! The other feminine heavenly body, the
Moon, fares equally badly. From the word lunar,
belonging to the Moon, lunatic and lunacy derive, both of
which have to do with madness or insanity! Sudden
misfortune is blamed on the heavens – the word disaster,
French *desastre* (astre=star), comes from 'astron', the
ancient Greek for star. Even our days of the week belong
to the planets. Sunday is the Sun's day, Monday, the
Moon's day (French *lundi*), Tuesday (French *mardi*) is
Mars' day, Wednesday (French *mercredi*) Mercury's day,
Thursday (Italian *jovedi*, French *jeudi*) Jupiter or Jove's
day, Friday (Latin *dies Veneris*, German *freitag*) Venus, or
her Norse equivalent, Freyja's day, and finally Saturday,
Saturn's day. When the seven-day week was established,
there were seven known planets (for this purpose the Sun
and Moon are included, although technically they are a
star and a satellite respectively). Now there are three
more, Uranus, Neptune and Pluto. Maybe astrologers
should campaign for a ten-day week. On second thoughts,
the present one seems quite long enough!

ASTROLOGY, THE ROYAL ART

Astrology was for a long time considered a 'royal' art. The kings of Babylon had attendant astrologers, so did Roman emperors. The latter didn't always treat their astrologers well. Emperor Tiberius, who dabbled in astrology himself, was not always delighted with the readings of his astrologers. If he didn't like their predictions, which he used to get the better of his rivals, he simply had the offending astrologer thrown over a cliff into the sea. In Chaucer's day, astrology was part of everday language. In *The Canterbury Tales*, for instance, the wife of Bath blames her amorous nature on the placement of Mars in her horoscope, in the earthy sign of Taurus. John Dee, sixteenth-century court astrologer to Queen Elizabeth I, chose her coronation date and advised against marriage with reference to her birth chart. Nostradamus became astrologer to Catherine de Medici and another sixteenth-century astrologer, William Lilley, predicted the Great Fire of London in 1666. Lilley drew up around 2,000 charts a year and in 1649 wrote the first astrological column in a newspaper. Astronomers Copernicus, Kepler, Brahe and Sir Isaac Newton were all court astrologers. John Flamstead, the first Astronomer Royal, was also an astrologer and actually chose the astrologically appropriate time for the founding of the Greenwich Observatory. Up until the seventeenth century astronomy and astrology were one and the same thing, like chemistry and alchemy. Sadly, astrology declined in popularity. Many abused its insights for propaganda purposes or financial gain. With the advent of the scientific revolution, anything that could not be measured and proved mathematically or scientifically was suspect and dismissed as superstition. As a consequence astrology suffered and finally disappeared from educated and intellectual circles.

ASTROLOGY TODAY

Astrology, considered by many to be a mere medieval superstition, has obstinately refused to remain in the closet. In the majority of daily and evening newspapers there is the ubiquitous Sun sign column. Many popular magazines devote a whole page or two to astrological forecasts. Newspaper and magazine astrologers receive literally thousands of letters a year. In autumn 1987, the first national screening of a regular astrology programme in the United States took place. Despite the sophistication of our rational, fast-moving, twentieth-century, high-tech existence with its emphasis on scientific truths, popular astrology flourishes. Or perhaps because of it.

It is interesting that, although we have been taught to acknowledge truth only in what can be proved by 'objective' science, many people find that there are still dimensions of their lives which cannot be explained rationally. Astrology provides us with a symbolic system which fuses the inner and the outer, the spiritual and the material. It gives us a meaningful framework within which we can try to understand the part we play in our mind-boggling cosmos of infinite time and space. It is perhaps through astrology that one of the bridges between rational science on the one hand, and intuitive belief on the other, can be constructed.

In recent years there has been a greater emphasis on astrological research. The fascinating work of the Gauquelins has already been cited (p. 18). Another researcher, Dieschbourg, studied particular pairs of planetary aspects in the charts of writers, painters and sculptors, and scientists, and found the results to be highly significant. The odds on the writers' aspect occurring were 10,000 to 1 against, and the painters and scientists were 1,000 to 1. Some astrologers, fed up with being dismissed as cranks by the scientific establishment, are using valid statistical methods to challenge their critics. Others are using astrological insights in the caring professions of counselling and psychotherapy. In this particular field, the work of psychologically orientated astrologers like Dr Liz Greene, inspired by the work of Swiss psychologist Carl Jung, has considerably enriched the interpretation of the natal chart for many astrologers, myself included.

Astrology is used, on a more 'mundande' level for stock market analysis, commodity trading and weather forecasting. The Israeli Secret Service, Mossad, used astrology to time the successful raid on Entebbe airport. Indian politicians are well known for using astrology, as do a number of western industrialists. British astrologer Dennis Elwell wrote to the directors of the P & O shipping company before the tragedy that befell the *Herald of Free Enterprise* in March 1987 to forewarn them. What prompted this action was a similarity between the pattern of the heavens at that time and the one which occurred when the Titanic sank. Unfortunately, the missive fell on deaf ears. Also in his excellent book, *The Cosmic Loom* Dennis draws some fascinating parallels between planetary patterns and the timing of IRA attacks.

In May 1988 former White House Chief of Staff, Donald Regan, spoon-fed the world's press with a juicy astrological story. We were told that Nancy Reagan actually consulted an astrologer who, after studying both the President's and Mr Gorbachev's charts, advised on propitious dates for US-Soviet summits, as well as fixing other daily engagements. Just as Donald Regan, in disclosing such information, implied that the President was out of touch with reality, so newspaper articles naturally extended the implications by inferring that astrologer Joan Quigley even had a hand in Reagan's policies. She was, however, merely advising on the precise timing of engagements in the presidential calendar and was in no way professionally involved in the engagements themselves. As I shall emphasise throughout this book, timing is one area where astrology can be very helpful.

SO WHAT IS ASTROLOGY?

Astrology is a symbolic system in which the planets and stars, and their movements, are seen to correspond with phenomena and happenings on earth. This ancient doctrine of correspondences teaches that there is a correlation between the heavenly and the terrestrial – as above, so below. It implies that an interconnectedness underlies all things in our universe. It offers a holistic view of reality. Astrology combines a scientific, astronomically correct, plotting of planetary movements with a philosophy of a unified universe and an art of interpretation. An analogy can be drawn with the earth's ability to maintain stable conditions for the whole living world despite a 25 per cent increase in the output of heat from the sun. The evolution of living organisms cannot be seen as a process which is separate from the evolution of our physical and chemical environment. We change with our environment and our environment changes with us. On a larger scale, the earth can be seen to have the same relationship of interdependency and interconnectedness with the rest of the solar system. The parts cannot be separated from the whole, like those of a three-dimensional hologram, illuminated by a laser beam. If the holographic plate gets broken, each of the fragments retains an image of the whole hologram.

The idea that there is a dialogue between earthbound humans and the heavens has been in existence since the time of sixteenth-century physician, Paracelsus. He saw us as universes in miniature, weaving a two-way pattern as we move through time. All this may sound very mystical, but there are so many things we simply cannot explain. No-one understands, for example, what happens after death, or why the 12-year-old son of a couple who both left school at 16 is already taking A-level maths and English literature. Even great scientists like Albert Einstein, the epitome of the rational thinker, hit upon the theory of relativity while gazing up at the sun through half-closed lids, daydreaming on a sunny afternoon.

Kekule, another scientist, solved the problem of how to arrange carbon atoms in benzene via a dream. He dreamt of a snake holding its own tail and suddenly realised he could arrange the carbon atoms in a circle, the benzene ring. To understand something of the world in which we live, we do need to be aware of the intuitive and the irrational, as well as the scientific and rational dimension. We need to combine the left or logical side of our brain, the part which is verbal and analytical, with the right or intuitive side which has to do with imagination and imagery. The astrological model does just that. When astrologers draw up a chart, or map of the heavens, they use precise astronomical tables and work out mathematically the planetary positions for a particular time and place. Then the chart is interpreted using the language of myth and symbol within the framework of a theory of correspondences.

SOME PLANETARY CORRESPONDENCES

In chapter 4, I will examine the symbolism of the planets more closely. Just to whet your appetite, here are some correlations involving some of the planets. The Sun is at the heart of our solar system and, like a heart, pulses in a steady rhythm. As recently as 1960, astronomers discovered that the Sun can be divided into four sectors through which the solar wind blows. This seems to mirror the structure of the human heart, with its four ventricles. Astrology also assigns particular metals to the planets. The Sun's metal is the most precious of all, gold. In her book *Astrology, A Psychological Approach*, Eve Jackson cites the interesting fact that gold, when taken internally on medical prescription, tends to gather in the body around the area of the heart. We say of a particularly good or kind person that he or she has 'a heart of gold'.

Mars, the red planet, is associated with the god of war and his metal is iron. Iron has long been used to make weapons, but what is even more fascinating is that we now know that there is iron on the surface of the actual planet.

This iron, combined with oxygen in the form of ferrous oxide, rust to you and me, whirls around on the surface of the planet in giant dust storms, giving it its red colour. The astrological symbol for the planet Mars is ♂ – the sign denoting male. Men do in fact have more iron in their blood than women. Women, on the other hand, whose symbol is ♀, the same as the astrological symbol for the planet Venus, have more copper in their blood than men. Copper has been associated with the planet Venus since ancient times, long before it was known that it circulated in the blood. The psychedelic colours of the planet Jupiter are caused by the continuous lightning discharges in its atmosphere. This is remarkably reminiscent of Jupiter or Zeus, the king of the gods, hurling down thunder and lightning from the top of Mount Olympus.

Analogous to these intuitive associations and their subsequent validation by modern scientific research are the theories of the old, traditional herbalists like Culpeper, who was also a practising astrologer. Many herbalists used to prescribe herbs according to the doctrine of similars which meant, broadly speaking, that where herbs grew or what they looked like indicated which ailments they could cure. The Lungwort lichens, on account of their pouched, lung-like appearance, were recommended for chest disorders. In point of fact, modern scientific research into the constituents of the species has revealed the presence of antibiotic chemicals which are indeed effective against chest infections. Lungwort continues to be prescribed by herbalists to this day. Our ancestors, without the benefit of our modern technology and knowledge, do seem to have known exactly what they were doing.

SO WHAT HAS ALL THIS TO DO WITH ME?

The answer to this is: a great deal. Let's come back to earth and examine the subject, called natal astrology, which looks at the correlations between the planets and events in the lives of individuals. This is the study of the natal chart or horoscope, a map of the heavens for the moment of birth. Whether we are aware of it or not, the correspondences I have been describing operate throughout our lives, correlating with the movements of the planets. The picture at the time of birth tells us a great deal about how we are likely to process experience. It gives us an insight into the cast of characters that make up the whole person we call ourselves. Some of these characters get along well, others conflict, sometimes violently. As American poet Walt Whitman said, 'Do I contradict myself? Very well, I contradict myself. (I am large, I contain multitudes.)' By looking at the qualities of the moment we came into being, and by analysing and interpreting them using the special language of astrology, what is within us can be seen in relationship to what is outside. The birth chart gives meaning to the patterns of experience we observe happening in both our past and our present. To understand why certain patterns repeat, especially those that have not been productive, we need to get to know ourselves better. The key word here is relating. How do I relate to other people? How do others see me? What part do I play? These are questions on which astrology can offer guidance. To understand the world in which we live, we would do well to begin by trying to understand ourselves. A modern psychological approach to astrology recognises astrology as a tool for living. Seen in this light, the birth chart is the means by which we can become more aware of not only who we are, but who we are in the process of becoming.

3.
A JOURNEY ROUND THE BIRTH CHART

This book is concerned with natal astrology – the study of the chart for a particular moment in time unique to you, your birth. The birth or natal chart is also known as the horoscope, from the Greek, *horoscopos*, meaning 'watcher of the hour'. The Greeks used this word to describe the Ascendant (see below), but it has now come to be applied to the whole chart.

WHAT IS A BIRTH CHART?

A chart is a landscape which describes a particular moment in time, seen from a particular place. Each passing moment is unique, possessing a special quality which draws together those ideas, events, phenomena, which are in tune with that moment. A person born at a particular point in time coincides with the chart drawn up for that precise moment, and at that place. Like a film running through a projector, the particular frame in which we make our grand entrance, is frozen. Our particular pattern is set, but that doesn't mean the chart remains a lifeless two-dimensional picture. As we grow, the chart grows with us, responding to the cycles of the planets. What we choose to make of this pattern is, to a certain extent, up to us.

A birth chart is rather like an ordnance survey map which tells us about the lie of the land. Parts of this landscape are smooth, green and fertile; other areas seem to be full of steep, stony paths which always follow the longest route. But as anyone who has walked with the aid of this type of map will tell you, it is only a guide to the landscape – it cannot tell you what the country looks, smells, and feels like, or how it changes with the light. The map is not the country. When we get out, map in hand, we know that we are going to walk in a certain area, but we haven't a clue who or what we might encounter on the road. Some of us seem to be better equipped for our journeys in terms of a start in life. The time at which we were born may have been a time of peace and economic prosperity; our home environment may have been loving, warm, and comfortable; our parents may have lived a harmonious life and encouraged us to express ourselves. Some of us, who were not so fortunate in terms of time, place, family, and environment, have still set out, hoping for better things. This reminds me of a strongly Capricornian friend who, though not as fit as his fellow travellers, was the only person in the party to get to the top of Mount Kilimanjaro. With the characteristic determination of this cautious sign, he summoned all his self-discipline and desire to succeed, and step by step, he made it: Capricorn isn't the sign of the goat for nothing!

The birth chart, then, expresses an inherent potential. However this potential does not exist in a vacuum, it has to be seen in context. Using the chart as a helpful guide, we interpret the symbols, as we would those in the key to a map. These symbols, which the signs, angles, planets, aspects, and houses, represent, tell us a great deal about how we are likely to process our life experiences and how we are likely to react. Yet there is still a certain indefinable quality which we will not find in the chart – that mysterious element common to all of us which is perhaps best described as soul or essence. Astrology cannot show the whole of our being or provide all the answers. I am not sure that anything can. However, rather than turning our brains into knitting wool, it might be more productive to forget about the answers and concentrate on the business of living; to get back to basics and 'to cultivate our garden' as Voltaire advised. The chart is a practical tool which many have found helpful in weeding their own particular patch.

Let us now look at the different components of the birth chart. It is not the intention of this book to show you how to draw up a chart. There are already many books available to teach you this, or you can refer to the appendix to find out where to learn astrology. Instead what follows is an introduction to the structure of the chart and its main features.

The chart shown here belongs to Virginia Woolf. She was born on 25 January 1882 in London at 8.45pm. It is impossible to attempt an adequate analysis of Virginia Woolf's chart in a few paragraphs. A satisfactory study of the complex themes contained within it deserves at the very least a whole chapter. However it is possible, by way of introduction, to draw attention to some of the chart's principle features and show how these are confirmed by what we know of Virginia Woolf's character. Her chart reveals an emphasis on the sign of Aquarius, since not only

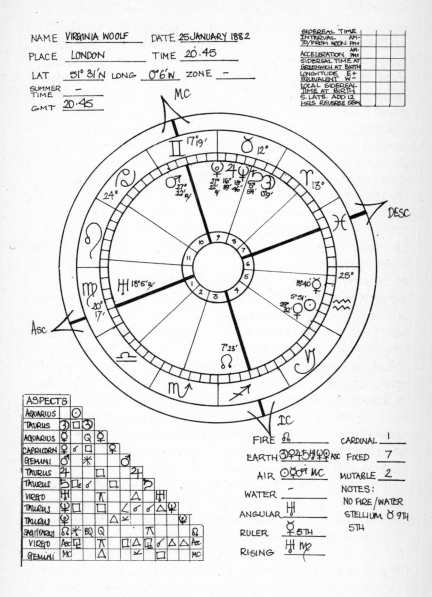

NAME VIRGINIA WOOLF   DATE 25 JANUARY 1882

PLACE LONDON   TIME 20·45

LAT 51° 31'N   LONG 0°6'W   ZONE —

SUMMER TIME —

GMT 20·45

SIDEREAL TIME		
INTERVAL AM- TO/FROM NOON PM+		
ACCELERATION AM- PM+		
SIDEREAL TIME AT GREENWICH AT BIRTH		
LONGITUDE E+ EQUIVALENT W-		
LOCAL SIDEREAL TIME AT BIRTH		
S. LATS. ADD 12 HRS REVERSE SIGN		

ASPECTS

AQUARIUS	☉												
TAURUS	☽	□	☽										
AQUARIUS	☿		Q	☿									
CAPRICORN	♀	☌	□		♀								
GEMINI	♂		✳			♂							
TAURUS	♃			□			♃						
TAURUS	♄		Ⅼⅽ	☌		□							
VIRGO	♅			⊼					♅				
TAURUS	♆	□			∠	⌄	☌	△	✳	♆			
TAURUS	♇			△	⌄				△		♇		
SAGITTARIUS	☊	✳	BQ	Q		·		⊼				☊	
VIRGO	Asc	Ⅼⅽ		⊼		□	△	Ⅼⅽ	☌	△	△	Asc	
GEMINI	MC		△			⌄			□		□	MC	

FIRE ☊

EARTH ☽♀♃♄♅♆♇ Asc

AIR ☉☿♂ MC

WATER —

ANGULAR ♅

RULER ♀ 5TH

RISING ♅ ♍

CARDINAL 1

FIXED 7

MUTABLE 2

NOTES:
NO FIRE/WATER
STELLIUM ☿ 9TH
5TH

is it her Sun sign but Uranus, the sign's planetary ruler, is
prominently placed on her Ascendant. Aquarius is an
independent, rational and progressive sign concerned with
social issues and the rights of the individual. Uranus can
signify a rebellious and unconventional personality.
Virginia Woolf, as clearly demonstrated by her book *Room
of One's Own,* understood the importance of personal
space and independent means for creative self-expression.
Without the benefit of the further education offered to her
male contemporaries, she achieved literary recognition at
a time when few women possessed either the means or the
confidence to write. Highly intellectual and forthright in
her opinions, she rebelled against the prevailing Victorian
patriarchal attitudes in a series of polemical feminist
writings. Her relationships were distinctly unconventional
in that her sex life with Leonard Woolf after their
honeymoon was virtually non existent, and she later fell in
love with a woman, Vita Sackville West. And she was, of
course, a member of the exclusive and unorthodox
Bloomsbury set. Her writing was often experimental
in form, and, in keeping with the rather sexless nature of
Aquarius, she strove for an androgyny of style which was
neither masculine nor feminine.

The Aquarius/Uranus emphasis also indicates a certain
coldness. This is further emphasised by the inhibiting
action of the planet Saturn in Virginia's chart on the
'feminine' planets, the Moon and Venus – they are
concerned with nurturing, feeling and relating. Virginia
Woolf could reasonably be described as both cut off from
her feelings and detached from the physical and the
sensual. Sexually unresponsive in her relationships she
admitted to not 'feeling enough' on her mother's death,
and periodically refused to eat. This denial of the 'earthy'
side of her character – she has seven planets and the
Ascendant in earth signs – took its toll on her mental and
emotional health. Her rigid self-discipline, shown by the
difficult aspect between the Sun in Aquarius and Saturn
in Taurus, left little time for relaxation. She wrote solidly,
every day, and took little time off at weekends. In

addition, the restless nature of Uranus which sits on her self-critical Virgo Ascendant implies a particularly highly-strung personality. Mercury, planet of communication and the chart ruler, makes a stressful aspect to Pluto indicating the potential for compulsive and destructive thinking.

WHICH IS MY SUN SIGN?

The dates given below are a general guide to the movement of the Sun through the twelve signs. You may find that in the book or article you have read, the dates may vary by a day or at the most two days. This need not worry you unless your birthday lands on one of those days which fall annoyingly between two signs, like 20 May which is right at the end of Taurus and almost at the very beginning of Gemini. This is generally known as being on the 'cusp' and many believe you have some kind of choice between the two Sun signs, taking a little of one and a little of the other or, even more convenient, choosing the one which most appeals! Our 20 May person may feel Taurus moves a little too slowly and opt for the more agile Gemini. Rest assured, you are definitely one Sun sign or the other, and this can be determined by looking up the exact date and time the sun moved from Taurus into Gemini. For example, in 1961 if you were born after noon on 21 May, your Sun sign would be Gemini. However on the same day in 1962, the Sun was still in Taurus, especially if you were before noon. Confused? Why not get your chart drawn up professionally? At least you will not have to go on wondering which Sun sign to own up to at parties and, on a more serious note, you will also get to know which of the other signs are important in your chart and see the picture as a whole, rather than dividing it, and yourself into separate parts.

Aries	♈	21 March – 19 April
Taurus	♉	20 April – 20 May
Gemini	♊	21 May – 20 June

Cancer	♋	21 June – 22 July
Leo	♌	23 July – 22 August
Virgo	♍	23 August – 22 September
Libra	♎	23 September – 22 October
Scorpio	♏	23 October – 21 November
Sagittarius	♐	22 November – 21 December
Capricorn	♑	22 December – 19 January
Aquarius	♒	20 January – 18 February
Pisces	♓	19 February – 20 March

In simple terms, the twelve signs of the zodiac, each occupying 30 degrees of the 360 degree circular chart, tell us in what way, or how, the planetary energies operate within us. Broadly speaking, a sign is emphasised if there is a planet or planets occupying its sector in the chart, or if it is our Ascendant (rising sign). The signs where we find the Sun, Moon, and the Ascendant (see below), are especially important. (There is much more about the signs in Chapter 5.)

THE ELEMENTS – EARTH, AIR, FIRE, WATER

Each sign belongs to one of the above four elements. In the Middle Ages, people believed that health and temperament were determined by the proportion of the four 'humours' or bodily fluids found in each individual. These are roughly analogous to the four elements and we still use the expressions today – people are described as melancholic (earthy), sanguine (airy), choleric (fiery), and phlegmatic (watery). This basic typology is used in modern psychology, for example by C.G. Jung, who postulated that everyone fell into four categories of temperament, these being thinking, feeling, sensation and intuition. Whilst the four elements do not exactly match these psychological types, the very fact that this fourfold division has survived for so many centuries is an indication of its value. Above all, as Liz Greene writes in her book *Relating*, 'Understanding something of this basic typology is an excellent way of learning that most difficult of lessons: that not everybody is the same as I am.'

Signs of the same element share a common feature. On one level, there is an understanding. However, the ten planets in the birth chart do not divide exactly by four, so one, or two, elements are always going to dominate. We usually have one 'leading' element which colours our personality and one with which we are not so comfortable. We describe people as 'being in their element'. Sometimes we do not have a single planet, or our Ascendant, in the signs belonging to a particular element. One friend with no planets in the earthy signs is a trained archeologist. He got in touch with his missing element by coming, quite literally, down to earth. I know of more than one psychotherapist with no planets in the watery signs, yet water is the 'feeling' element! It seems that we are often drawn to what we lack or, as someone once said, 'We teach best what we most need to learn.' There is a more detailed study of the elements in Chapter 5 which deals with each of the twelve signs, grouped according to element, but for the moment, a general summary of each element and the signs belonging to it should suffice.

The Element of Earth – Taurus, Virgo and Capricorn

Those of us who are attuned to the element of earth generally feel comfortable in the physical or material world. We are 'grounded' and in touch with our bodies. We enjoy eating, sex, and other sensual pleasures, and relate to the outside world via our senses. Earthy types do not usually find money or responsibility a problem. We prefer to base our knowledge on concrete experience which we assimilate and digest in a kind of organic process, before forming an opinion. Earth signs are not afraid of commitment, and once we have embarked on our chosen course we persevere, only changing direction when it has been proved that this is the most realistic course of action.

Our motivation is born of a need to preserve and maintain. Sometimes such dogged perseverance leads to obstinacy and failure to see opportunities, especially those which involve taking risks. We need to be aware of the necessity of letting go when something has run its course. Following a routine may be secure but it can blind us to alternative possibilities and could lead to loss of freedom or even our *joie de vivre*. Taureans can dig in their heels when threatened and refuse to budge; Virgo can organise life to the point where anything which doesn't fit into the grand pattern is rejected; Capricorn is notorious for a brand of conservatism which makes many sacrifices for the sake of conformity.

Too little earth, or a denial of the earth element as seen in Virginia Woolf's chart, which has seven planets plus the Ascendant in earth signs, can manifest itself in a distorted image of the body, not feeling at home in our bodies, and paying too little attention to physical needs. Virginia Woolf was both anorexic and sexually unresponsive. We all need earth to keep our feet on the ground and stay in touch with the steady natural cycle of growth.

The Element of Air – Gemini, Libra, Aquarius

Those of us who are predominantly airy types are at home in the realm of ideas. We perceive the level on which things relate to each other and form connections. This necessitates an ability to stand back and take an objective stance so that we can look at things from different angles. This reflective quality of air is a civilising influence – we are not simply at the mercy of our instincts. Those of us who operate through the element of air are good with people. We can take into account someone else's point of view and be fairly diplomatic. Just as air needs to circulate freely if it is not to become stale, airy types need room to manoeuvre. Airy types prefer to keep their options open, not being comfortable in situations where there is no element of choice. We tend to be rational thinkers with a philosophical bent, capable of objectively assessing a situation.

It is this objectivity, however, that can lead to indecisiveness and lack of real involvement, since we can appreciate many different points of view. Unlike the earthy types, air does not find commitment easy. Gemini's conversation is characterised by phrases like 'Yes, on the one hand ... but, on the other hand'; Libra is usually to be found sitting on the fence; Aquarius stands well back, avoiding anything too personal or 'heavy'. Too much air results in dissipation of energy. The goods never are delivered through indecisiveness or not taking into account the practical or the personal dimensions of life. We can be accused, quite rightly, of 'living in our heads'. Virginia Woolf, with three personal planets in air signs, took refuge in a life of the mind. With too little air in our charts we may be prone to making sweeping generalisations. Often we fail to consider the implications of our actions so that we find ourselves embroiled in situations or relationships we later regret. Air gives us mobility, perspective and lightness.

The Element of Fire – Aries, Leo, Sagittarius

Fire warms and can be shared. Those of us with an emphasis on the fiery element infect other people with our warmth and energy. We need to get things moving, make things happen. Our essentiallly optimistic outlook on life results in a positive attitude and expression. Things tend to come our way because of this kind of creative visualisation. If you believe things will work out for the best, there is a good chance that they will. This may seem a little naive to the other three types, but the vitality and spontaneity of fire has a wonderful habit of ensuring we are in the right place at the right time. We are interested in possibilities, in what the future has in store, and for this reason make good entrepreneurs or initiators. We can encourage and motivate others, seeing obstacles not so much as drawbacks but as challenges to be overcome. Fiery types are often at home in areas where we will be noticed, like on the stage, running our own organisations, or standing up in front of a classroom or lecture theatre.

We can, however steam ahead without thinking, or noticing who we have trampled on the way. Aries is well-known for rushing in, head first, not stopping to think. Leo has a reputation for a rather child-like need to be the centre of attention. Sagittarius can all too easily preach instead of teach. If we have an over-emphasis on the fire signs we can literally burn ourselves out, like a forest fire, leaving a trail of destruction as a result of our rash and careless impulses. Too little fire can manifest as a lack of enthusiasm and self-confidence, blocked energy, and a rather pessimistic attitude to life. Fire brings trust, energy and a positive outlook.

The Element of Water – Cancer, Scorpio, Pisces

Water responds. Those of us with a preponderance of this element in our charts are feeling types. We need involvement, especially on a personal level. Our responses to people, situations or events are not based on theories or conscious evaluation. We simply know whether something feels right or wrong. We allow impressions to filter through, tuning in to atmospheres and how other people are feeling. We need other people for our emotional well-being, and we also like to be needed. Watery types see life as tidal, always ebbing and flowing from the same source. Water can change shape to fit any container and watery people can be equally changeable. We can appear mysterious to the more rational air signs who can't seem to pin us down. Water has to do with nuance and subtlety; those of us who operate from this watery feeling level can be perceptive, sometimes to an uncannily accurate degree.

Our sensitivity and vulnerability, however, can lead to our being hypersensitive and emotionally at sea. Cancers are reknowned for getting their claws in and not letting you go. Scorpio can be very intense, loving you or plotting your downfall with equal passion. Pisces can be chameleon-like, both saviour and betrayer. Feelings, however, have their drawbacks if we are unable to switch off. Too much water may result in our being water-logged. We need others yet tend to live through them, finally driving them away through our demands and over-reactions. Too little water, on the other hand, can lead to denial of feelings – the stiff upper lip syndrome – breeding loneliness and isolation. Then, when our repressed feelings eventually surface they seem uncontrollable. Virginia Woolf's chart reveals a complete lack of planets in the water signs. Water helps us to feel the flow, and go with it.

CARDINAL, FIXED AND MUTABLE

The twelve signs are further divided into the above three qualities, known as the 'quadruplicities'. They indicate ways of acting and reacting.

Cardinal Signs – Aries, Cancer, Libra, Capricorn
Cardinal equals action and these signs like to get things started. Those with an emphasis on this group of signs are self-motivating and enthusiastic, directing their energy into schemes and projects. Cardinal signs take the initiative: Aries has the vision, Cancer the feelings, Libra the contacts, and Capricorn the strategy. All four signs love to be involved in something, or their energy is lost to them.

Fixed signs – Taurus, Leo, Scorpio, Aquarius
The fixed signs implement and maintain what the Cardinal signs have begun. They move at a slower but determined pace and make dependable friends and partners. You can always count on the fixed signs: Taurus offers physical comfort, Leo loyalty, Scorpio emotional support, and Aquarius sound advice. Old habits die hard and the fixed signs tend to resist change.

Mutable signs – Gemini, Virgo, Sagittarius, Pisces
The mutable signs possess the flexibility lacking in the fixed signs. They adjust and respond to new ideas and surroundings. Mutable signs love change and find it easy to adapt to different circumstances: Gemini has the mental agility, Virgo is versatile and practical, Sagittarius

visualises the potential, and Pisces' responds to subtle changes in the atmosphere. The mutable signs are not predictable; they are consistently inconsistent.

THE PLANETS

Sun	☉	Hero/Heroine, Creator, Initiation and Integration
Moon	☽	Mother, Nurturer, Instincts and Responsiveness
Mercury	☿	Communicator, Connector, Cunning and Intelligence
Venus	♀	Lover, Beauty, Attraction and Relationship
Mars	♂	Fighter, Instigator, Energy and Drive
Jupiter	♃	Seeker, Teacher, Expansion and Optimism
Saturn	♄	Realist, Controller, Structuring and Boundaries
Uranus	♅	Awakener, Inventor, Vision and Individuality
Neptune	♆	Artist, Mystic, Idealisation and Union
Pluto	♇	Transformer, Eliminator, Power and Possession

The planets are arranged round the chart rather like the cherries in a cake or the pips in an orange. Some slices have no pips or cherries, others have more than one. The planets embody principles or energies which work from within. They are the dynamic forces which function in all of us, whether consciously or unconsciously. We will discuss each of the planets in Chapter 4, but for the moment it will serve to think of them as personifications of instincts such as the urge to relate (Venus) or to communicate (Mercury). The sign in which a planet falls tells us how its energies will operate. For example, if your Venus is in the sign of Taurus, the sensual and the physical side of a relationship will be important.

THE HOUSES

You will see that the chart shown (p. 45-46) is divided into twelve segments which sometimes straddle more than one sign. These 'houses' are like the segments of our orange which contained the planets. There are twelve of them and they tell us where the planetary energies, modified by the signs, are acted out. The boundaries between the houses are called 'cusps' with the Ascendant (see below) always the cusp of the first house. Each of the houses can be likened to a series of theatrical stage sets or even different aspects of a house you might inhabit. The setting of our dreams is often a house and this is a well-established image of our life-situation. We are all familiar with the kitchen or living room, but sometimes we discover that the house has a mysterious, dark cellar or a cobwebbed attic, hitherto unexplored. The fourth house, for example, represents our roots so could be the basement, while the third house deals with the area of communication so could be the place where we write, use the 'phone, or watch TV. To know more about which particular areas feature strongly in your life you will need to have your chart drawn up professionally. As a basic guide, the themes of the houses with the sign which is most at home in that house are:

First House Aries	Where we meet the outside world; image; the front door.
Second House Taurus	Security; resources; the safe- deposit room or where we hang the Picasso!
Third House Gemini	Communication; mental attitude; the writing/phoning/TV/word processor/ computer room.
Fourth House Cancer	Roots; childhood; the basement, the kitchen or the nursery.

Fifth House Leo	Creativity; play; the studio or games room. Virginia Woolf's chart shows three planets in this house, the house of creative self-expression.
Sixth House Virgo	Health and habits; attitudes to work; the room with the desk, and filing cabinet; the bathroom.
Seventh House Libra	Partnerships; awareness of other people; our next door neighbours.
Eighth House Scorpio	Emotions and sexuality; the bedroom.
Ninth House Sagittarius	Exploration; education; religion; the study. Virginia Woolf had five planets in this house. Her writing is exploratory and adventurous in form, content and style. She also taught and lectured.
Tenth House Capricorn	Status; aspirations; the house we'd really like to own!
Eleventh House Aquarius	Groups; social concerns; the local pub or community centre.
Twelfth House Pisces	Seclusion; unconscious elements; skeletons in the closet.

THE ASCENDANT

Some of you may already be familiar with this term, which is also known as the rising sign. Along with the Sun and the Moon, it is one of the three most important components of the birth chart. It shows the exact degree of the sign of the zodiac which is rising over the eastern horizon at the time of birth. The Ascendant proclaims our entry into the world, our first breath. It marks the beginning of our particular life cycle. Each sign of the zodiac is divided into 30 degrees and the time and place of our birth determine the exact position of the Ascendant within that sign segment. Since this point, or angle, of the chart marks our collision with the outside world, it is an important and sensitive area. Just as you alter the focus on a camera or change the lens in order to get a good shot, so the Ascendant is the lens through which we look at reality. I like to use the analogy of a shopkeeper looking out through the shop window. To you, the passer by, he or she is simply a seller of whatever the shop supplies. To the shopkeeper you may be a potential customer. In reality both parties have other roles in life, but we tend to see people in context. The sign on the Ascendant shows both how we perceive the world and other people, and how they in turn perceive us. Think of someone wearing dark glasses on a winter's day. They may want the edge taken off the stark light of day for a reason – they may, for example, have a dreadful hangover. You, on the other hand, may think that they are particularly pretentious, or wonder if you just passed a famous rock star in the street. Getting to know our Ascendant can often explain why people seem to read us wrongly. We know better than they what sort of person lurks behind the image, but we cannot expect others to see the whole of us. To go back to the camera analogy, we choose what we want in the picture and how much light to let in through the aperture.

Imagine you are at a party. The person with Leo rising will wait for the right moment and make a grand entrance while the less self-assured Capricorn will grab a drink and try to look as inconspicuous as possible. The Scorpio rising is probably the one wearing the dark glasses and no-one can get a word in edgeways while the Gemini rising is around. The Cancer rising has probably made sure everyone knows where the food is while the perfect host or hostess, always diplomatic, probably has Libra rising. All of these rather stereotyped characters have many other facets to their personalities but it is often the Ascendant which comes across first. It colours our perception of other people, and vice versa.

Sometimes one of the planets is near the Ascendant on the birth chart. This modifies the expression of the sign considerably. For example, our confident Leo rising may be positively pushy if Mars, planet of action and assertion is placed on the Ascendant. By way of contrast, the nurturing instincts of our Cancer rising may be severely hampered by Saturn, planet of caution and discipline, and manifest in lack of confidence and awkwardness. Virginia Woolf had Uranus prominent on a Virgo Ascendant, intensifying the restless, analytical nature of this mentally orientated sign.

PLANETARY ASPECTS

Just to recap, the planets are dynamic, inner forces whose essential expression is modified by the sign in which they are placed on the chart. The houses show those areas of life in which the planets express their energies most strongly. Last, but by no means least, the planets form aspects to each other, calculated geometrically within the 360 degree circle of the chart. These aspects, which can involve more than two planets at a time, mean that the planets concerned are engaged in a dialogue. Some aspects are harmonious, others produce a certain amount of tension. Some planets, by their very natures, such as the more feminine or 'yin' Moon and Venus, get on well together.

If we go back to our own personal cast of characters for a moment, some are going to hit it off from the beginning, others may get involved in a family feud which could last for years! By getting in touch with the alliances formed between the members of our inter-planetary family, we can see which of these relationships need a little more effort and encouragement. Some, of course, will always get on like a house on fire, and we regard these as our strong points, or the things which come to us most naturally. We all have both sorts of aspects, the flowing and the tense, in our charts. Some of us do seem, however, to have more family feuds than others. Yet often, a preponderance of easier planetary relationships can make us complacent, while those which seem conflicting or stressful may motivate us to take up challenges and reap the ensuing rewards.

CHART RULER

This term is applied to the planet ruling the sign on the Ascendant of the chart. Virginia Woolf's chart ruler is Mercury since her Ascendant is Virgo. If her Ascendant had been Capricorn, the chart ruler would have been the planet Saturn.

4.
THE PLANETS

The birth chart is an astronomically correct picture of the
heavens at a unique moment in time, as seen from a
precise location on the earth's surface – our birthplace.
From our terrestrial point of view, the Sun appears to
circle the earth, travelling along a path known as the
Ecliptic. The Moon and the other eight planets appear to
accompany the Sun, moving in formation along this same,
but wider, route. This broader path extends between 8°
and 9° degrees on either side of the Sun's course and is
called the zodiac. (I shall be discussing the twelve signs of
the zodiac in the next chapter.)

Although modern astrologers look a the solar system
from an earth-centred or geocentric point of view, we are
perfectly aware that the Sun is the centre of the solar
system. And, in case you were worrying, we are not
members of the Flat Earth Society! No astronomer can
fault the standard tables we use to plot the planetary
positions, but the notion that the Sun moves round the
earth is patently absurd. Quite so, but astrology is a

symbolic language. It is concerned with how the planetary patterns and their links with the signs and houses operate in our lives here on earth. Our inner universe is a mirror image of the perceived universe, out there. We live our lives on earth 'as if' we were at the centre of the universe.

EARTH

The Great Spirit is our Father, but the Earth is our Mother. She nourishes us; that which we put into the ground she returns to us, and healing plants she gives us likewise. If we are wounded we go to our mother and seek to lay the wounded part against her, to be healed.
      Bedagai, or Big Thunder, North American Indian, early 1900

It has always puzzled me that many people seem to take the fact of our planet's continued existence for granted. Many astrologers, their sights set firmly on the cycles of the other heavenly bodies, seem to have developed short sightedness when it comes to our planetary home. The philosophy underlying astrology supposes that the universe is a moving, seamless whole. If we sympathise with this supposition, then planet earth, on which we live, is an equally important part of that whole. Although the earth does not appear on the birth chart and is therefore not interpreted in the same way as the other astrological symbols, I would still like to acknowledge the miracle of this living planet.

When we look at the famous photograph of the earth taken from outside its atmosphere, we can appreciate what a beautiful blue and white pearl we inhabit. The sight deeply affected astronauts looking at earth from the Moon. They felt part of it and underwent a profound shift in perspective. James Lovelock's Gaia hypothesis acknowledged the earth as a living being engaged in a constant cycle of supporting and maintaining life. Plants alone, whether on land, or as sea algae, enable us to breathe, through photosynthesis – when they breathe out, we breathe in. In the same way as the human body maintains a steady temperature or a chemically balanced blood supply, planet earth ensures that environmental conditions are just right for our continued survival.

Gaia was the Greek goddess of the earth. In the beginning, according to the classical Greek poet, Hesiod, was the vast darkness of Chaos, then came Gaia who gave birth to Uranus, the starry sky. So the universe came into being. Gaia and her son, Uranus, united to create the Titans and their offspring, and the population of the world began. Earth, from whom all things were created, was the first deity or Great Mother in many primitive cultures. She was usually represented as a large, rounded woman, a symbol of fruitfulness and nourishment.

Since the 1960s, awareness of Mother Earth as a living entity has blossomed. The ecology, peace, alternative medicine and wholefood movements are testimony to this shift in consciousness. It is interesting that in the early 1980s, concern for the potential destruction of our race and our planet by nuclear weapons was voiced most vigorously in Britain by a group of women, at Greenham Common. The feminine principle, symbolised in one sense by a more responsible attitude to our planet's resources and the emergence of more natural ways of living, is re-awakening from a long sleep.

PLANETARY SYMBOLISM

Astrology is a system in which the Sun, Moon and the other eight planets are seen as forces which combine in a moving pattern to shape our lives. These planetary energies are modified according to their relationship with each other in the chart, and according to the signs and houses in which they fall. When looking at the planets in your chart it is helpful to think of each of them as one of the cast of characters in your own particular television series. These characters have markedly different attributes and some want to hog the stage when you would rather they had been written out of the series, or at least

that particular episode. Those personalities whose parts
we have tried to edit out have a habit of making their
presence known whether we like it or not, and sometimes
in the most inappropriate scenes. Perhaps we have all
much to learn about writing scripts and directing. A
well-rounded, true-to-life drama would allow space for all
those characters within us to express themselves. The
aspects of ourselves, or sub-personalities, which we have
cast in starring roles, will seem much less one-sided if we
also try to write in a few cameo roles for those characters
we are secretly embarrassed by. Hopefully, the production
as a whole will be richer, more interesting, and ultimately
truer to ourselves.

PLANETARY ENERGIES

The planets taken as a whole sybmolise the drives and
patterns of behaviour through which we each express our
own individuality. These forces are common to all of us,
but the way they are arranged around each individual
birth chart and their connection to the signs and houses is
an indication of our uniqueness. We are all special and
astrology treats us as such. Another useful way of
describing the planetary energies is to think of them as
archetypes. This term comes from two Greek words:
arche, meaning beginning, and *tupos*, meaning figure or
image. An archetype, therefore, is the original pattern or
model – it is a key image, present from the beginning,
which shapes our perception. A good example of an
archetype is Mother. This single word is
multi-dimensional – it may bring to mind our own mother,
an ideal mother, someone else's mother, or even a religious
image like Da Vinci's 'Madonna and Child'.

The planets as archetypes are very much alive in all our
psyches. Our ancestors personified them as gods and
goddesses which were common to all cultures, albeit with
different names. Nowadays we regard these ancient belief
systems as unsophisticated mythologies. We know there
are no gods living on the top of Mount Olympus in Greece.

However these powerful images have stubbornly taken root within us. They appear in dreams and in works of art. They surface in everyday life. Those colourful figures, who catch our imagination, especially among royalty, film stars, television personalities and politicians, are often the modern counterparts of the gods and goddesses, heroes and heroines of ancient civilisations, or even characters from fairy tale and legend. Marilyn Monroe is a case in point. She was, for many people, and especially men, the living personification of the ideal woman, a love goddess. Heroes of popular culture, like Clint Eastwood, are flesh and blood embodiments of the virile warrior archetype, pursuing heroic fantasies on the silver screen.

Every culture updates existing mythology while simultaneously creating new variations on an old theme. It is the image presented by particular people in the public eye which furnishes us with an appropriate hook on which to hang our own version of a mythic figure. This is of paramount importance in understanding such cultural archetypes. We are not taking into account the person as a whole, just that aspect of them which corresponds with our fantasies. In the same way, the gods and goddeses, heroes and heroines of myth and fairy tale are not rounded characters but personifications of forces, drives, energies and instincts.

The planetary names in current usage are drawn from Greek and Roman mythology, since the invasion of Europe by the Roman armies ensured the survival of their language, culture and mythology. A brief exploration into myth and legend from Graeco-Roman and other cultures furnishes valuable material for a richer understanding of the planetary principles at work in the birth chart.

THE SUN

Rules: the sign of Leo and the fifth house

The Sun, technically a star and not a planet, has a kind of atomic furnace at its core which generates a massive output of fiery energy. Scientists have studied the surface activity of the Sun, but so far it has not been possible to penetrate its interior. It is the pulsing heart of our solar system, kept in exquisite balance by its self-regulating nuclear centre. Our human hearts mirror the Sun's function by pumping blood and maintaining a constant temperature in our bodies. Like the heart, all life is dependent on the Sun's steady cycle of light and warmth. Without the Sun, plants would be unable to convert carbon dioxide into oxygen or provide us with the bulk of our daily food.

In astrology, the Sun is perhaps the most complex of all the planets. Popular Sun sign astrology has, however, done most of us a disservice by grossly oversimplifying the essential meaning of this planet. As astronomers have already found, we cannot see into the Sun. The astrological Sun, modified by sign, house and aspects, represents both the guiding light on our journey of self-development and the journey itself. For many of us, this means first getting to like and accept our Sun sign. You would be surprised how many people wish they had been born under a different sign of the zodiac. I have trouble with this myself!

In Egyptian mythology, the Sun was personified as Ra, the creator. He ruled peacefully while young and strong but, weakened by age, he was lifted up into the sky on the back of the goddess Nut, there to ride his boat across the sky during the twelve daylight hours. Lying in wait on Ra's daily journey from east to west lurked his eternal adversary, the great serpent Apep, who lived at the bottom of the Nile. In times of solar eclipses, Apep succeeded in swallowing the solar boat, but it always reappeared, Ra having banished the serpent back to the watery depths.

In Greek and Babylonian mythology we find similar

motifs. Helios, the Sun, drives his fiery chariot across the sky as does his Babylonian counterpart, Shamash. Apollo, the beautiful and youthful Sun-god, also has to do battle with a serpent, Python, a female dragon-monster into whose cave he wanders and whom he despatches with an arrow.

The Sun, then, is a creative principle, usually personified as masculine, and a heroic figure with a starring role. Its energy expresses itself most naturally in the sign of Leo, the traditional sign of rulers or heroes. In astrology the Sun symbolises our centre, our inner light. Like Ra's and Apollo's journey's, the process of self-development may necessitate battles with monsters in various guises, but the heroic dimension of the Sun symbolises potential strength and awareness. The Sun is essentially 'masculine' in the sense that strength, courage and the other attributes of the mythic hero have been traditionally identified with masculine or 'yang' energies.

Such solar attributes, however, also have a negative dimension. Unbridled strength or sheer arrogance can be destructive, showing up on the birth chart as difficult aspects to planets such as Mars, Uranus or Pluto. To go back to Egyptian mythology, the awesome power of the hot Sun resulted in much of the land being arid desert, dependent on the annual flooding of the Nile to render some of it fertile. Set, the god who personified the desert, was a violent, murderous god, the eternal adversary of his brother Osiris who represented the fertile earth, the life-giving river Nile, light and creativity.

As a 'masculine' principle, the Sun in the birth chart can often signify our image of the father, or authority figures in general, and tell us much about how we experienced our personal fathers. Women have equal access to solar energy, although many of us find it difficult to express our strength or creativity with sufficient confidence. However, many people have experienced their mothers as the strong, active force in the family so the Sun in the birth chart does not always describe the father. In Celtic myth the Sun or fire was represented by a goddess, and the German word for Sun is feminine.

The Sun in astrology indicates a way of potential integration. It symbolises a journey we are primed to make, with dragon fights included. On another level it can signify our true vocation, as opposed to our profession. We all begin life with a birth chart within which the Sun is the most important living symbol. In one sense, however, outside influences such as family, environment, the times we live in, combine to dim its glow. Not until we have gained some measure of insight into the kind of person we are growing into, which for most of us can only be grasped after we have reached approximately 30 years of age (see Saturn), do the diverse characters that combine to make a whole personality begin to solidify. This long journey may lead us back to the beginning, but along the way we might find ourselves and, as in T.S. Eliot's famous words, 'know the place for the first time'.

THE MOON

Rules: the sign of Cancer and the fourth house

The Moon and the Sun are two opposing principles which together form a pair. In the Chinese yin and yang symbol, the two halves of the same circle contain a fraction of their opposite. This symbol represents the polarisation and reconciliation of two opposing functions. Yang, which originally described the sunny side of a mountan, is the masculine principle – bright, hot, high, penetrating and dry. Yin, the dark side of the mountain, is the feminine principle – dark, cool, deep, receptive and wet. The ancient Chinese philosophy of Taoism saw the universe as a moving web and used the complementary opposites of yin and yang to explain the continuous process of natural change within it. So, the Moon is a yin symbol, and the Sun, yang. Without the Moon, the Sun would have no means of reflecting back his brilliance, while the Moon's softer, reflected light illumines the night sky after the Sun has set. The Moon's gravitational pull on the earth is responsible for tides, as well as the level of sap in green

plants and the feeding habits of marine creatures such as
oysters. There is a connection between lunar cycles and
bleeding, as women have always known. I was once given a
'lunar-menstrual' calendar and was fascinated to discover
that menstruation occurred naturally just before or
sometimes on the exact day of the full Moon. One study
carried out in 1980 found that the majority of women
menstruated at either the new or the full Moon, rarely at
the first quarter or the last quarter. We cannot prove the
connection between the Moon and bleeding, but the two
have always been associated and women may find this
helpful.

In astrology the Moon is a feminine planet which is a
symbol of containment, belonging and receptivity. As a
container the Moon is associated with our bodies, which
contain us, and our mothers who carried us in early life.
Whereas the Sun's yang energy is forward looking, the
Moon leads us back to our childhood, our roots, or
the place where we felt safe. The Moon's sign at birth,
together with aspects to the other planets and house
position, tells us much about our instinctual nature. This
is the non-rational part of ourselves that is motivated by
those basic needs which can often seem very un-adult –
the need to be comforted, or fed, or looked after. When we
respond instinctively to a person or a situation,
automatically, without first thinking about what to do or
say, then we are operating from what astrology terms our
lunar side. The Moon represents the line of least
resistance where we are easily hurt. It is a kind of
emotional anchor which has to adjust to cycles of growth
and change. In reality the Moon has a calm interior
producing only a ten-billionth of the tremors undergone by
the earth in a year. It reflects the light of the Sun,
generating no energy of its own. Often, the element of the
Moon's sign at birth shows how we defend ourselves in
emotionally charged situations. The Moon in the fire signs
(Aries, Leo, Sagittarius), will fight; in the water signs
(Cancer, Scorpio, Pisces), become tearful; in the earth
signs (Taurus, Virgo, Capricorn), show resistance or

become stubborn; and in the air signs (Gemini, Libra, Aquarius), argue or try to reason.

When we look at the mythological personifications of the Moon, however, the image of the Moon as Mother is not the planet's only dimension. The Moon in the sky also has a dark side upon which we never gaze, as it is forever turned away from the earth. It is also sometimes obscured by clouds, and constantly changes shape. In Greek mythology three goddesses are associated with the Moon, according to its three phases. Artemis is a lunar virgin huntress who was so outraged when the mortal Actaeon saw her bathing naked that she set his own hounds upon him to rip him to pieces. Hera, queen of the gods, represents the full Moon, a woman fulfilled as a wife and mother. Hecate, an underworld divinity, is the waning Moon, a dark, mysterious crone or witch with magical powers and a retinue of infernal hounds. Isis, the Egyptian goddess who had a large cult, was partly a Moon goddess. She was a healer, magician, courageous and ultimately victorious in her battles with the wicked Set. She even persuaded, by rather devious means, the great god Ra to reveal to her his secret name. So, the Moon also has a dark face which can be powerful, mysterious and intimidating, not least to men. A far cry from the idealised, nurturing mother.

In the same way that the Sun at one level represents Father, the Moon can shed some light on our image of Mother, and indicate how we experienced our personal mothers. Fathers who had a markedly nurturing, more 'yin' feel are often represented by the astrological Moon. Indeed the Babylonians worshipped a male Moon god, Sin, and as children we anthropomorphize the Moon as the Man-in-the-Moon of nursery rhymes. Difficult planetary aspects to the Moon indicate vulnerability, a sense of being without self-protection. Lunatic, from the Latin word for moon, means insane or mentally unsound and is used to describe those who cannot cope with reality. It was formerly applied, according to the dictionary, to 'the intermittent kind [of madness] attributed to changes of the Moon'. Harmonious lunar aspects, on the other hand, help us to feel more comfortable – with ourselves and others – and less exposed to threat, whether on an emotional or a physical level.

MERCURY

Rules: the signs of Gemini and Virgo, and the third and sixth houses

Whereas the Sun and the Moon represent the polarities of masculine and feminine or yang and yin, Mercury is much more difficult to pin down, especially in terms of gender. The ruler of Gemini, like that sign's symbol of two pillars, has a dualistic nature which can be both male and female, old and young, honest and dishonest.

A good analogy for Mercury is the human brain – highly appropriate for this fast-moving planet which represents the urge to communicate, connect and classify. Our brains have two sides or hemispheres, left and right. The left brain, corresponding to the right side of the body, processes information in a logical, linear, sequential manner; it is predominantly involved with rational, analytical thinking and controls our speech. The right brain, corresponding to the left side of the body, enables us to recognise faces, signs, orientate ourselves; it synthesises and relates information, rather than breaking it down, and enables us to move our bodies around. On a practical level we read and interpret symbols, like 'No Entry' signs, with our right brain, and process information such as 'Maximum speed 70 mph' with our left brain. Both are necessary if we are to make any sense of our environment.

In Greek mythology Hermes (Mercury in Latin) was the messenger of the gods, carrying news to and from the gods and between gods and mortals. Statues portray him as a youthful god with winged sandals. Swift, like our thought processes, he was also the god of traders, travellers and thieves. His mischief-making was apparent from the day of his birth when he stole his brother Apollo's cattle, driving them backwards so that their hoof-marks would not give away their direction. After eating two of them, he was brought before Zeus, the king of the gods. Zeus was so amused by the child's cunning, he did not punish him but simply ordered the cattle to be returned.

Hermes was also an accomplished pursuer of nymphs and fathered numerous children by them. This playful aspect of Mercury is readily seen in those with a strong emphasis on the airy sign of Gemini. His earlier Egyptian counterpart, Thoth, was a wise, older man, patron of all the arts and sciences, inventor of medicine, mathematics and, especially, writing. This grounded aspect of Mercury corresponds more closely to the earthy sign Virgo which sorts and analyses information in order to put it to use. Thoth was also spokesman and scribe of the gods, and possessed magic texts with alchemical formulas to transform man and nature. Hermes' other main function, as Hermes Psychopompus, was to lead the souls of the dead to the underworld. So, he had access to the world of humans, the divine heights of Olympus and the dark nether regions of Hades, the only god with such flexibility of movement.

Mercury is the nearest planet to the Sun and in astrology his function is to build bridges between inner and outer, seeing and understanding, irrational and rational. Mercury symbolises our need to make sense of our world, the urge to understand and communicate. As the Sun's messenger, Mercury, god of travellers, can be both a help on our journey and a hindrance if we refuse to acknowledge connections such as those between actions and consequences. Mercury's slippery nature is evident in those who live on their wits and cunning, or those who mislead by giving out double or contradictory messages. Yet sharp wit can be a source of great pleasure, and we admire those mercurial types who juggle words effortlessly, always ready with a witty riposte, even if it is at someone else's expense. The more tongue-tied among us also have Mercury in our charts but perhaps in a water sign or in difficult aspect to the planet Neptune. This may indicate a more intuitive, less factual way of thinking which is Mercury in right-brain manifestation. A friend with such a feature on the birth chart recently plucked up the courage to attend a public speaking and communications course, in search of both confidence and clarity of expression. One way of contacting Mercury is to write down your dreams – you may be surprised at your hidden talent for puns and visual word-plays. For example, dreaming of spoons may mean you are doing a bit of stirring!

VENUS

Rules: the signs of Taurus, Libra, and the second and seventh houses

Venus in astrology symbolises our urge and capacity to relate. She represents the power of attraction between opposites which is often sexual in nature. The placement of Venus in the birth chart indicates our capacity for relating, or where we experience problems in relationships. It reveals how we would like others to relate to us, or what we find beautiful. Venus in her Libran aspect is more comfortable with aesthetics – appreciative of art, culture and good taste in a rather detached sense. The Taurus face of Venus, on the other hand, is earthier and indicates a love of nature, making love, eating well, luxury and pleasurable physical sensations generally.

Venus in the birth chart can also symbolise what we value and how we value, or undervalue, ourselves. The energy of Venus can express itself in highly creative ways. A love of beauty, nature and harmony can be expressed in many manners, from the creation of an easy, harmonious atmosphere to a work of art.

In mythology Aphrodite (Venus in Latin) was the goddess of love. She was born in the sea from the foam of her father Uranus' severed genitals, and, as depicted in Botticelli's celebrated 'Birth of Venus', carried to the shore in a huge conch shell. This, however is an idealised

portrayal of a chaste Venus. The Aphrodite of Greek
legend was an arch seducer of men, both gods and mortals
– even Zeus succumbed to her charms. Later statues of
Aphrodite were modelled on the voluptuous figures of
courtesans, and it is this sensual, sexual aspect of the
goddess which gave us words like venereal. It is
unfortunate that the word in common use is now
synonymous with sexual disease. It originally meant 'of
sexual intercourse'.

Ishtar, or Inanna, the Babylonian equivalent of
Aphrodite, was the most popular goddess in Assyria and
Babylonia. A strong, passionate goddess she was kind and
compassionate, even helping mortals. Hers was the
vitalising, vibrant energy of attraction which inspires
sharing and involvement with others. Yet there is a dark
side to Aphrodite. The Greek goddess made her lame,
blacksmith husband Hephaestus miserable with her
numerous affairs, and would not tolerate any competition.
She was said to delight in inspiring women to
uncontrollable passions, sometimes with tragic results.
The planet Venus is aptly described as 'torrid' since
temperatures there rise to 900°F and the enormous
atmospheric pressure has crushed many research
spacecraft. Venus-inspired passions can lure us, like the
mythical sirens, on to the rocks.

Venus, in a woman's chart symbolises her relationship
to her own femininity and sexuality; in a man's it
represents an ideal image of woman as a lover. Through
Venus we can find out more about what we value, and how
we value ourselves. Hard planetary aspects to Venus, such
as those involving Saturn, can indicate poor self-image
and self-esteem. This can result in the 'ugly duckling'
syndrome of undervaluing ourselves which can cause
problems in relationships. A well-placed Venus bestows a
loving nature, a sense of self-worth and the ability to make
people feel they matter. Venus in the water signs likes
relationships with depth; in the air signs loves to be
civilised and hates coarseness; in the earth signs needs
physical demonstrations of love; in the fire signs looks for

passion and panache. We look to Venus, on one level, for whatever turns us on – or off!

MARS

Rules: the signs of Aries and Scorpio, and the first and eighth houses

Mars is the red planet and symbolises direct, unadulterated energy. The glyph, or symbol, astrologers use for Mars is the biological sign meaning male. Like this sign which is phallic or weapon-like, Mars' energy is dynamic, thrusting, sharp and decisive. Red signifies heat and danger and Mars supplies heat in the form of energy, adrenalin and drive. Dangerous situations bring out our survival instinct, the 'fight or flight' response to stress. Sports champions in the Gauquelin (see pp. 18–19) study had this planet prominent in their charts and we would expect similar findings in the charts of thrusting entrepreneurial types, martial artists or those who enjoy a challenge. Mars is that side of us which asserts our will over that of others so that we get what we want. In true decision-making we have to separate off from others and Mars, as a counterbalance to the relating urge of Venus, helps us to express what we desire. The Aries side of Mars is the hot-headed, courageous and competitive spirit, embodied by many warrior heroes, like the Samurai. The Scorpio side is the primitive survival mechanism we all possess, that enables us to fight to defend ourselves and what is ours. The planet Mars has two moons named after the attendants of the god of war – Phobos and Deimos, meaning fear and panic. If we are afraid, doubt ourselves and panic, we cannot tap Mars' energy and become stuck, lacking the courage to make a move.

Ares (Mars is his Latin name) was an unpopular god of war, the embodiment of blind rage and brutal courage, enjoying nothing but strife and battles. Like his mother, Hera, Zeus could scarcely control him. Ares' impetuous nature lost him many battles. It also landed him in Hephaestos' net whilst he was making love to the blacksmith's wife, Aphrodite. Ares' sister, Athene, the Greek warrior goddess, was a much cooler, more intelligent figure. She was born, fully armed, from the head of Zeus, and protected heroes such as Hercules and Perseus. She guided Perseus in his confrontation with the gorgon, enabling him to cut off the monster's head.

Mars, Ares' Roman equivalent, enjoyed greater popularity and we see in him a more productive side of the god of war. He was originally a god of vegetation and fertility whose major festivals fell in spring. As protector of agriculture and animals, he represented the creative impulse towards growth, the impetus of the seed to sprout. Only later was Mars associated purely with war.

The mythology surrounding Mars broadens and enriches our understanding of this inner planetary force. If we can express and focus our energy we are unlikely to be walked over. Assertiveness is not necessarily destructive, but blind rage is. If we can direct the urge towards self-preservation and growth, symbolised by Mars, then our enterprises have more chance of coming to fruition. We find it difficult to harness our energy where there are difficult aspects to Mars, say from Neptune. Energy can be dissipated and ultimately lost to us. Another problem is blocked energy which can show up as difficult aspects to Saturn in the chart. This energy may turn inwards to reappear as migraines or backaches or any one of the symptoms now associated with stress. Undiluted Mars is uncontrollable and destructive rage. We can see in our own times the dark face of Mars in the destructive potential of nuclear fire power towards humans and nature. In Greek myth Ares and Aphrodite were lovers. If pure Mars energy is balanced by Venus, the two principles vitalise each other and their fusion can be creative.

The planets we have met so far are called the 'personal' planets and represent those inner drives which manifest on a personal level in our lives. Jupiter and Saturn, the next pair, take us outside ourselves. They represent the urge to look beyond our immediate situation and, from experience, learn how far we can go.

JUPITER

Rules: the signs of Sagittarius and Pisces, and the ninth and twelfth houses

Jupiter, with its twelve attendant moons, is the largest planet in the solar system. Its mass and volume are more than one and a half times as great as all the other planets combined (excluding, of course, the Sun which is a star). Jupiter's brilliant colours are the result of huge atmospheric lightning discharges, befitting a planet named after the god of thunder and lightning. Jupiter symbolises the urge to free ourselves from limitation, broadening our horizons, both physical and mental.

In Greek myth Zeus (Jupiter in Latin) was the son of Kronos (Saturn), a father who was in the habit of devouring his children at birth, because an oracle had predicted he would be overthrown by one of them. Luckily, and luck seems to be connected with Jupiter, his mother, Rhea, tricked her husband Kronos into swallowing a stone instead and Zeus was brought up in secret. Later, with the help of his regurgitated brothers and sisters, he did indeed overthrow Kronos to become the great Olympian patriarch.

Zeus was married to Hera, queen of the gods, but had an insatiable appetite for women, both mortal and goddesses. As the great fertiliser, he was not averse to employing all manner of disguises such as a swan and a shower of gold, or resorting to violence, to satisfy his desires. Zeus fathered a prodigious number of children since every one of his unions proved fruitful, yet he remained bound to his wife. The chase was paramount – Zeus was not looking for long-term commitment. He is depicted as an ample, imposing, bearded, avuncular figure, emanating authority and with a wise countenance. When angered he hurled down thunderbolts from Mount Olympus, like Thor the warrior god of Teutonic myth. Zeus is the supreme god, worshipped on high, all-seeing, all-knowing. Although a faithless husband he was a wise and compassionate ruler.

Jupiter in astrology has much to do with seeking. This can take the form of travel and exploration, or philosophical and spiritual development. This planet is connected to our quest for meaning, the faith and optimism which perceives a pattern and a purpose to life. We can turn the adage 'where there's life, there's hope' into 'where there's hope, there's growth' to encapsulate Jupiter's essence. The principles of expansion and extroversion belong to Jupiter, and it is not surprising that this planet figures prominently in the charts of actors, especially those who excel at declaiming from the stage in classic Shakespearean roles. Jupiter is traditionally a planet associated with luck. Certainly, if we approach life with the essentially optimistic and confident attitude associated with a well-placed Jupiter, then we stand a good chance of getting what we want. Jupiter is said to rule the liver. The word jovial (Jove=Jupiter) conjures up an image of a jolly, rounded, avuncular figure who may indeed have liver problems because of an over-fondness for food and especially drink.

The negative side of Jupiter, however, is much less attractive. Like the lofty arch-seducer of Greek myth, we may literally 'go over the top', puffed up with our own self-importance. As a law unto ourselves and bent on satisfying our own desires, we become self-centred and conceited. This aspect of Jupiter reminds me of the frog who wanted to be as big as an ox in Aesop's fable – an ego that has got out of hand cannot expand forever. However, we all have Saturn in our charts and his sobering influence helps to keep Jupiter in check!

SATURN

Rules: the signs of Capricorn and Aquarius, and the tenth and eleventh houses

Saturn was the furthest known planet until the discovery of Uranus in 1781. Encircled by rings of light, Saturn has ten moons, the largest, Titan, being comparable in size to the planet Mercury. Astrologically Saturn symbolises the need for boundaries, order and form, beautifully represented by the planets own outer rings. Physically Saturn is said to rule both the skeleton which gives our bodies form, and the skin which marks our frontier with the world and other people. Saturn is connected with lessons learnt, with duty, responsibility, hard work and self-discipline. It is immediately apparent from this rather kill-joy set of characteristics why the ancients called Saturn the Greater Malefic and identified him with the Grim Reaper. Saturn has definitely had a bad press since, psychologically speaking, the placement of this planet on the birth chart indicates those areas where we feel inferior, vulnerable and fearful. However, the process associated with Saturn is that of learning through experience, and also of trusting time. Phrases such as 'Time is the great healer' have Saturn's ring of truth.

I have already mentioned Kronos (Saturn in Latin), the child-swallowing father of Zeus/Jupiter, who was a Titan, an earthy god whose own father, Uranus, was so appalled by his ugliness that he was crystallised and imprisoned in the earth. Kronos, however, took his revenge for this rejection by castrating Uranus and succeeding to the throne he coveted. However he sat uneasily on this throne, paranoiacally eating his own children in a vain attempt to control his destiny, which proved ultimately self-destructive. He was then banished to the underworld.

Another version of the myth tells a different story. The Roman Saturn was a happier god who ruled the Golden Age when man lived in harmony with the earth. His reign brought prosperity and agricultural abundance. His seven-day festival of Saturnalia in December, which predates our Christmas celebrations, was a period of unrestrained feasting at which masters served their slaves, and when law courts were closed. Pan, another figure associated with Saturn, represents sexual abandonment, lechery and the fertility of nature. In medieval times this cloven-hoofed and horned figure was synonymous with the devil, serving as a warning to good Christians against the sins of the flesh.

From the mythology associated with Saturn two things are apparent. Firstly, it is both unwise and unproductive, like Kronos, to resist change. Secondly, if we are patient, realistic and trusting, there will come a time, like the Saturnalia, when roles are reversed and we can throw off our inhibitions. In the birth chart, Saturn is potentially a wise teacher, although his lessons may be hard. As an earthy, reality principle Saturn's influence is more apparent after the planet has come full circle around the birth chart. This does not happen before our 29th birthday (and again around age 58) which is usually when we see the consequences of our previous actions and decisions (or lack of them), and take stock of our situation. If Saturn is emphasised in the birth chart we like to be in control, of ourselves and of the situation. We may also be fond of positions of responsibility and authority, especially those where we find ourselves in control of other people or finances. If we have not made a friend of Saturn, we can feel inferior, socially awkward, and find spontaneous expression difficult. On the positive side, Saturn teaches the value of realism, perseverence and determination to succeed. A good example of such determination is Margaret Thatcher who was born with Saturn on the Ascendant.

THE OUTER PLANETS

Beyond the orbit of Saturn lie the slower moving 'outer' planets. In meaning they embody the essence of the historical epoch in which they were discovered. Since they move more slowly through the solar system than the previous seven planetary bodies, whole generations have the same planet in the same sign. For example, Pluto remained in the sign of Leo for almost twenty years which means that everyone born approximately between August 1938 and July 1957 will have Pluto in Leo in their birth chart.

URANUS

Uranus was discovered in 1781, an era of social upheaval
and rebellion. America was fighting for independence from
Britain and 1789 marked the beginning of the French
Revolution. Both revolutions, in which the underprivileged
revolted against those in power, had worldwide
repercussions. Social hierarchy lost some of its rigidity – a
step on the road towards the ideal of the classless,
egalitarian society – and the struggle for the freedom of
the individual began. This was also the dawning of a
technological age. The invention of new technology, most
crucially of steam power in 1769, forced dramatic changes
in the British social and economic structure.
Communication by electro-magnetic fields, the radio, was
soon to be possible. Herschel, who discovered the planet,
had a strongly individualistic streak. As an astronomer
and a musician he liked to rush back to his home-made
telescope in the intervals between performances at which
he was playing. Uranus is an individualist *par excellence*
among the planets. It has a very odd axis of rotation which
means that it circles the sun lying on its side and the
planet's polar regions are alternately exposed to 42-year
periods of sunlight and darkness.

Astrologically Uranus represents new ideas and
attitudes, the need for change and innovation. If we regard
Saturn as the great traditionalist of the zodiac, then
Uranus is the eccentric or revolutionary, cutting through
the barriers of convention. Uranus points the way to a
brighter future where individual freedom is of the essence.
This 'brave new world' is a vision, founded on innovation,
independence and rebellion against the status quo.
Today's iconoclastic or revolutionary attitude may become
tomorrow's orthodoxy, but then another Uranian flash of
revelation will illuminate the way forward.

Uranus, the elevated sky-god who banished his ugly
offspring from his sight, was finally overthrown by his son,
Kronos (Saturn). He was a remote and obscure god,
preferring to remain in the sky-world of divine truth and

light, rather than descend to the gross world of physical manifestation. Like Prometheus who stole fire from the gods to raise man above the level of animals, Uranus symbolises that foresight which can be uplifting. Prometheus' punishment, however, was isolation. Uranus has also been identified with the Teutonic magician-god Wotan or Odin. He was a shape-shifter, god of storm and the fury of battle. Society certainly did change shape when Uranus was discovered, and three of the planet's satellites are named after Shakespearean characters from the magical world of spirits and fairies – Ariel, Titania and Oberon. Radioactive Uranium was discovered eight years after the planet Uranus and this was much later to be used to split the atom, releasing a power which did in fact cause terrible storms and fury in battle – the atomic bomb.

Uranus, then, symbolises the urge to tear down the old and usher in the new. When this planet is strongly emphasised in the birth chart, we are open to new ideas and new technology. We may appear eccentric, espouse alternative views and lifestyles, and exhibit a marked independence of spirit. Taken to extremes, such an inability or refusal to fit in can result in loneliness. A possible example is Camus' figure of the 'Outsider', alienated from society like the sky-god and the mythical Prometheus. Yet Uranus is also connected with tolerant humanitarianism and social progress, as in the slogan of the French Revolution 'liberty, fraternity and equality'. An image for Uranus is the light bulb which flashes over our heads when we have a sudden blinding insight. Such inspiration can be a magically exciting awakening. It can also come as a frightening shock to the system, cutting through and ripping away our old, comfortable ways of seeing. Uranus needs space to express its energies most creatively or disruptions ensue. Where Uranus is concerned we must always expect the unexpected.

NEPTUNE

Rules: the sign of Pisces and the twelfth house

Neptune was discovered in 1846. Named after the god of the oceans and watery depths, this planet has many affinities with water, an extremely sensitive substance which in its pure form is colourless, odourless and tasteless. Water is also capable of adapting itself to a far greater range of circumstances than any other liquid. Scientists are not even sure exactly how it works. Indeed, in keeping with watery Neptune's uncertain nature, astronomical pictures of the planet show only a blurred disc, partly obscured by methane clouds. Six years before the official discovery of the planet, anaesthetics were first used. In this same historical period photography was born, culminating in the first roll film and box camera in 1888. Spritualism and eastern philosophies flourished, homes for the poor were established, and art entered a new Romantic period.

Astrologically, Neptune, like the sea, is linked with the unseen, the unfathomable and the mysterious. To Neptune's realm belong fantasy, dreams, imagination and illusion. If this planet is emphasised in the birth chart people may find us dreamy and vague. We tend to live in the active world of the imagination which can be both immensely creative and yet moodily escapist. Wherever Neptune falls in the chart we experience a longing for something glimpsed but elusive, like the perfect love. Through Saturn, we are aware of our boundaries – where I end and you begin. Neptune urges us to dissolve those boundaries and seek the kind of union associated with mystical or spiritual yearnings.

In the creation myths of many cultures, life came from water. The Babylonian sea-goddess Tiamat symbolised the primitive chaos of nature in monstrous form. In Babylonian myth she is represented as a great fish who threatens to swallow Marduk, the king of the gods. He manages to destroy her, and so organises the universe. Dionysus, originally god of wine, is a Greek god who also has affinities with Neptune. He asked that his followers sacrifice everything to follow him in the pursuit of ecstasy. On his travels, he had a habit of striking those who would not acknowledge his divinity with madness. Eventually he was torn to pieces by the Titans, but his heart was rescued and he was resurrected. He then became, like Jesus Christ, a symbol of everlasting life.

These mythic tales serve to illustrate the different faces of Neptune. As a creative energy, Neptune represents the source of inspiration and a private place where we can escape the narrow confines of reality. In Neptune's realm, the artist, the poet, the musician, and the romantic make their home. The artist in us can find meaning in expressing feelings or ideas through painting, photography, poetry and especially music. Such feelings do not translate into words. Listening to a piece of music needs no taped commentary. In matters of the heart we have all perhaps clung to the notion that somewhere there exists the perfect lover. Unfortunately these soul mates are hard to come by, and often when we think we have finally found our fairy tale prince, he has a nasty habit of changing back into a frog. If we fall victim to our fantasies, however, they can swallow us whole; especially if we try to block out reality with constant alcohol or drug abuse. Neptune symbolises the capacity to love unconditionally, to forgive and forget. People with this planet strongly emphasised tend to make sacrifices for those they hold dear. It can be difficult, however, to separate true sacrifice from giving up something to make another person feel guilty and obligated. Those with Neptune on the Ascendant may find they tune in like the dial on a radio and pick up other people's feelings. Such 'sensitives' might welcome the protective boundaries symbolised by Saturn, to avoid becoming psychic sponges.

PLUTO

Rules: the sign of Scorpio and the eighth house

Pluto, the outermost known planet, was discovered in 1930. It is faint and awkward to observe adequately, even with huge telescopes. The planet was named after the god of the underworld who was invisible when he came above ground. The 1930s saw the rise of Fascism, the power of American gangsters, advances in atomic physics, and growing acceptance of Freudian psychoanalysis. The common denominator in all these events is their link with the idea of the underworld – those energies which lie simmering below the surface and which erupted in synch with the discovery of the new planet. It is hardly necessary to point out that the atomic bomb's active component is plutonium, first produced artificially in 1940. Pluto represents the wealth that lies below the surface. Like oil, we have to dig deep and hard to reach it. Indeed, the pipeline which carried oil under the Channel to British troops in World War II was named Pluto. We may not, however, recognise what we find as in any way precious until we hold it up to the light, which transforms it. And then, of course, much depends on how we choose to use it. Pluto is also symbolic of those processes, like depression, which takes us downwards and inwards to hopefully resurface feeling much lighter, in both senses of the word.

Hades (Pluto in Latin), the Greek god of death who ruled the underworld, was as powerful in the nether regions as Zeus in the upper. Like the planet he is a dark, shadowy figure. He received buried treasure and only left his kingdom twice, once to abduct and rape Persephone who became his bride and the other time to cure a wound. His word was irrevocable and his decision final. Visitors to the underworld were unwelcome, they had to force their way in or, rarely, make a deal with Hades. In Sumerian mythology there was a goddess of the underworld, Erishkegal. Her most celebrated visitor was her sister, Inanna or Ishtar, Queen of Heaven. Inanna had gone down in search of her dead lover's body, but as she passed through the seven gates she was stripped, humiliated and finally killed and left to rot. In the end Erishkegal was persuaded to set her sister free. She was sprinkled with the water of life and began her ascent, recovering her clothes as she passed through the gates.

Pluto, like Hades, is a powerful force. When this energy erupts it can be violent, like the nature of Hades above ground. Astrologically, Pluto symbolises those powerful drives which, once we are in their grip, seem to take over completely. They include power-seeking, compulsive behaviour and obsessions. Pluto rules the eighth house which is traditionally associated with three notoriously problematic areas, namely death, sex and money. It is no coincidence that it is in precisely these realms that a great deal of obsessive behaviour originates. On a more positive level, Pluto, like Inanna's journey, represents the necessity of stripping away what has been outgrown and no longer serves any useful purpose. Unlike the snake which instinctively knows when it is time to slough off an old skin, many of us stubbornly resist change. Pluto indicates the wisdom of unloading some of the baggage we all carry around with us, and regularly clearing out our cupboards. Money and death are often connected – death can make people wealthy through inheritances, for instance. Psychologically and physically there are processes which necessitate difficult journeys, like depression and illness. When we re-emerge, we can take pleasure in a new sense of ourselves. In the process we may also have discovered our very own bit of buried treasure.

5.
THE SIGNS OF THE ZODIAC

Each person's birth chart contains all twelve signs of the zodiac. Even if we have no planets in a particular sign, it will still be activated as the first seven planets make a complete cycle through all twelve signs of the zodiac. The three outer planets travel at a slower pace. Some of us will experience a complete cycle of Uranus around the birth chart – it takes roughly 84 years. None of us will be around to witness the completion of either Neptune's or Pluto's cycles as they take approximately 165 and 248 years respectively. The speedy Moon takes just 29 days 12 hours and 44 minutes to move through the zodiac wheel while Saturn moves at a more sedate pace, taking between 28 and 30 years. So, although in our birth charts specific signs will be accentuated, we will still have the opportunity to experience the nature of the remaining signs when they are brought to life by the orbiting planets.

The description of the signs which follow are grouped according to element (for more about the elements – fire, air, earth and water – see Chapter 3). Just as the element balance varies from chart to chart, so your individual horoscope will carry an emphasis on one, two, even three signs. The signs in which the Sun, Moon and Ascendant are placed are especially important. It is rare for any chart to have all three in the same sign. Usually they fall in different signs, often of different elements. Everyone knows their Sun sign, but when you find out your Ascendant and Moon signs as well, magazine horoscopes become much more fun. That way you get to read three versions of what's going to happen to you that month!

By now you will have realised that there is no such things as a totally typical Leo, for example. Charts do exist with five planets in the same sign, but there are still the other five to consider, plus the Ascendant and the inter-planetary aspects. And the signs, unlike the planets, are not energies or forces. They are rather like filters through which the planetary light and energy are percolated. Sometimes there is harmony between the planetary principle and the character of the sign, and then the planet's energy comes through in a more concentrated form. Sometimes the planet's energy is diluted in some way. For example, the fluid nature of the Moon expresses itself much more naturally through the imaginative lens of Cancer than via the controlled filter of Capricorn. The descriptions which follow therefore, represent the pure, undiluted essence of each sign. In reality no-one will express ony the qualities of that sign, even if it is their Sun sign. Also the personalities of each sign 'type' have been deliberately exaggerated to convey more effectively that sign's particular meaning. Consequently, you will not meet anyone who completely fits any of the descriptions given in this chapter. Astrological typecasting is fun but, like any other sort, can only present stereotypes which are not true to life. We are all more complex than that. So why not read all the signs to get to know the unfamiliar aspects of yourself as well as the familiar. A good place to start is the sign opposite your Sun sign – it is often the one you can't stand!

THE FIRE SIGNS

Aries 21 March – 19 April

Aries is a cardinal fire sign. Its symbol, the ram, appears in Egyptian mythology as the ram-headed god Ammon – a phallic deity of fertility, representing the creative force. He was proclaimed king of the gods by his followers and was the patron of the most powerful and victorious pharaos. The name of one of the most famous Egyptian kings, Tutankhamun, means literally 'living image of Ammon'. Aries is the first sign of the zodiac which begins at the Spring Equinox. As on the first day of spring, we wake up ready to throw off our sluggish winter layers and sprout like a newly germinated seed.

Aries is the sign of beginnings. The Arien personality enjoys taking the initiative, challenges, adventures and risks. Charging headlong into the fray, competitive Aries, blessed with the essential courage and confidence of the fire signs, loves to win. Ruled by the planet Mars, fearless Ariens need an outlet for their eager energy. They certainly had their day in the Age of Chivalry when crusading knights performed deeds of bravery and valour whether for God, king and country, or fair damsels in distress. Warrior queens like Boadicea or tribes such as the Amazons demonstrated that courage and daring were not exclusively masculine traits. Present day Ariens, like Clare Francis who sailed the Atlantic single-handed, do battle with the elements. Martina Navratilova, whose Moon is in this sign, braves the fierce competition of the international tennis circuit. Strong-minded Hollywood stars Bette Davis and Joan Crawford, both Sun Aries, exemplify the energy and fiery temperament of this sign – the indomitable Ms Davis is still making films in her eighties. Other Arien women I have met cope with demanding jobs in competitive areas like publishing and advertising. In the workplace, Ariens like positions where they can make decisions and take risks. Challenges bring out the best in them. 'Go for it!' is the Aries motto. Great Britain is a pioneering, empire-building, Aries country with a dragon-slaying patron saint. In recent times this aggressive, Mars-like streak has manifested itself in the invasion of the Falkland Islands and the behaviour of our football fans.

Although Ariens can seem pushy, their direct, dynamic *modus operandi* can motivate and stimulate the more timid amongst us. Superb delegators, Ariens encourage self-confidence in others by giving them a chance to prove themselves. With Aries, what you see is what you get – nothing is hidden. Like the other fire signs, the simple faith of Aries, together with the warmth and generosity of the sign, tempers their often infuriating lack of patience. Like small children, they tend to live in the present, impatient for tomorrow's adventures. For Aries, the world is full of creative potential as they prospect for precious metals in their own personal gold rush. They thrive on action, feeling vaguely ill at ease on days like Sunday when the shops are shut and nothing much is going on. Warm-hearted Ariens bear no grudges. Defeats and setbacks are quickly forgotten as they pick themselves up, dust themselves down, and start all over again!

All twelve signs of the zodiac have a negative manifestation and Aries is no exception. Competitive, uncompromising Aries allows no-one and nothing to stand in its way. Those who have witnessed Aries in a temper or come too close to the Arien fire tend to get burnt. So does the Aries who makes no allowance for the mundane realities of huge overdrafts or credit card bills. Ariens are generally not to be found clearing up messes, even of their own creation. Their naive courage and creativity excuse them from such dull tasks which they delegate to others. Yet Aries' energy can burn itself out, especially when those with an emphasis on this sign persist in butting their heads, ram-like, against immovable obstacles. In relationships, impulsive Aries rushes in only to find the romance soon loses its fairy-tale dimension – 'Marry in haste, repent at leisure' will strike a chord with many an Aries. However, I have also encountered many Ariens who behaved more like Librans, refusing to acknowledge their need to assert themselves and meet challenges creatively. One Aries client with a prominent Venus, planet of relationship and harmony, always put others first. When prompted to confront his own needs, he was surprised at the amount of frustration and anger he had stored up. Aries needs to develop the capacity for compromise and co-operation of its opposite sign, Libra, but maintain a healthy self assertion. If we want beautiful roses in our garden, we must prune them. When positively expressed, Aries makes judicious use of the secateurs.

Leo 23 July – 22 August

Leo is a fixed fire sign. Its symbol is appropriately the lion, king of beasts, and its planetary ruler is the Sun. Majestic is a fitting adjective for this regal sign. Ancient rulers like the Pharaos, sons of Ra, the Sun god, identified themselves with the sovereign lord of the heavens. Leo is the hero or heroine, concerned with fulfilling his or her own destiny which can be mythical in dimension. Warm, loyal and steadfast, Leos believe that life will provide them with opportunities to demonstrate their qualities of rulership and magnanimity. The desire to create is strong and can take the form of a work of art, a business, or children. Interwoven through this creative fabric is the often unconscious desire to be immortalised in some way and many a Leo, when pressed, will admit to a sneaking desire to leave something of themselves to posterity. Napoleon Bonaparte was a Sun Leo.

Leo loves to shine, as befits a sign ruled by the Sun. Many Leos have something of the showman in their character like Cecil B De Mille. Strutting rock star Mick Jagger has a raw, leonine appeal – he has the Sun, Mercury, Jupiter and the Ascendant in Leo. Robert

Redford, dubbed Hollywood's 'golden boy' is another Sun Leo – more radiantly attractive and energetic than many men half his age. Leo needs to be somebody, and to have an effect on others. They take a pride in whatever they undertake and actively seek approval for their efforts, beaming like small children when praise is forthcoming. Leos love a bit of theatricality and showiness. One Leo friend's wedding was a real event – bride and groom left the church in an Indian rickshaw and the reception featured a theatre group dressed up as ancient, fumbling waiters plus country dancers and cannon fire! Even if on the surface the Leo personality does not make an immediate impact, given the opportunity they will rise to the occasion.

Idealists at heart, Leos cling on to their inner vision even when reality threatens to distort their rosy view of life. The open, generous and sunny nature of the typical Leo stimulates others to respond with equal generosity. Straightforward in manner, but with more tact than a typical Sagittarian, Leos are definite in their displays of both approval and disapproval. You know where you stand with a Leo who will be above all honourable in his or her dealings with you. Generous to a fault, you will always receive a warm welcome from Leos, whatever their means. Leos possess an innate faith and trust in humanity, a positive outlook which reaps rewards. Matthew Manning, one of today's most successful and scientifically tested healers, has six planets in Leo. He teaches positive visualisation techniques while all that Leo fire channelled through his hands literally burns away disease and pain.

The down side of Leo is not so pleasant. Those with this sign strongly emphasised in the chart can display an unquenchable thirst for personal glory. Their oversized egos need constant massaging and they are prone to 'lord' it over people who are less confident or talented. The Leo arrogance is well-documented and they do not like being upstaged. Granted they may well have style and charisma, but underneath they are mortal like the rest of us. Leos hold an unerring belief that they know what's best for you.

Their unstinting well-intentioned advice on how to run your life is, sadly, another manifestation of the Leo conviction that they possess a spark of what can only be termed divine insight. Unfortunately for them it comes across as a form of arrogance and only pushes those the Leo wants to help further away.

In relationships Leos can, perhaps unconsciously, choose partners who will enhance their qualities, providing a foil for their starring role. This is all very well until the partner begins to feel like an appendage, however lovable the Leo may be. Leo would be well-advised to cultivate some of the qualities of the opposite sign, Aquarius, like greater objectivity and consideration of others. One Leo client admitted that life was like a big toyshop and she wanted to sample as many goodies as she could. Unfortunately, there's no such thing as a free lunch and sooner or later Leo has to realise that he or she is as accountable as the next person. All children must grow up, but some Leos manage to hang on to their childhood well into middle age! When the radiant Leo vitality and innate trust is used to help and inspire others, it can fire the rest of us to get in touch with our own creativity.

Sagittarius 22 November – 21 December

Sagittarius is a mutable fire sign. Its symbol is the mythical centaur, half-human, half-horse, aiming his bow and arrow at some distant goal. In the character of Jupiter, planetary ruler of Sagittarius, we see many of the attributes of this sign. Imposing, dramatic, with a larger than life quality, Jupiter is always in hot pursuit of some new adventure, usually a female. Sagittarius is a big, expansive sign, capable of maintaining many irons in the fire as befits the volatility and versatility of a mutable sign. Fired by the quest, Sagittarians, ever optimistic, are apt to shoot as many arrows as high and as far into the air as they can. It doesn't really matter if they are way off target. What is essential to Sagittarians, as they canter off towards the distant horizon, is a colourful, exciting journey. Committed travellers, Sagittarians love to journey to foreign shores. Some, however, never leave their armchairs, preferring to expand their mental horizons by burying their noses in books or studying new subjects.

Sagittarius is associated with the ninth house of the chart, the house of the seeker, the wise teacher and philosopher. This aspiration towards meaning is a Sagittarian life theme which will be tackled with hope and enthusiasm. If Sagittarians have something to believe in, their natural optimism, coupled with the trusting nature of the fire signs, ensures that they land on their feet and usually in the right place at the right time. Launched into a quest for meaning, whether spiritual or philosophical in nature, the Sagittarian spirit seeks personal growth and, by extension, new developments in society at large. Teaching and journalism provide outlets for Sagittarian ideas. Progressive and open-minded, Sagittarians make stimulating teachers, drawing out their pupils and promoting lively debate. On a spiritual level, the Sagittarian search for faith ahd meaning is apparent in the work of the visionary poet and painter, William Blake, born with Sun conjuncting Jupiter in Sagittarius. For famous Sagittarian soprano, Maria Callas, music was her religion.

Above all, it is essential that the Sagittarian is given a free rein and a rolling landscape in which to gallop. Too long a period spent in the stables will only result in the Sagittarian making a desperate bolt for freedom, and you may never again catch them. Like their opposite number, Gemini, Sagittarians hate to be tied down. Film director and comedian Woody Allen, a Sun Sagittarius, prefers the space afforded by living alone, even though he is now a proud father. Unless there is a lot of Cancer or Taurus present in the chart, Sagittarians prefer the broad dimensions of the big screen or, like Maria Callas, the opera stage, to the cosy domesticity of the TV set.

As you would expect with such a larger than life sign, the Sagittarian faults are pretty glaring. Discussions can all too easily turn into heated arguments as the Sagittarian fires are kindled. Woundingly direct, the Sagittarian verbal arrows strike home whilst flying hooves deliver painful kicks. Tactless and lacking the sensitivity of the water signs, Sagittarius when threatened can turn dramatically antagonistic. The storm soon blows over as far as the Sagittarian is concerned, but others are left smarting. Jupiter did everything on a grand scale and Sagittarians, or those whose charts show an emphasis on that planet, are similarly prone to exaggeration of speech and gesture. Sagittarians dramatise their lives so they seem more reminiscent of scenes from grandiose operatic productions. With a fondness for sweeping generalisations to ensure the maximum dramatic effect, the Sagittarian speech is peppered with over-the-top phrases. Sagittarian actress and singer Bette Midler is notorious for her outrageous remarks. And so it is with Sagittarian emotions. In love, or fired with enthusiasm for a significant new project, the Sagittarian attains great heights. Unfortunately the lows which unavoidably follow, plunge the Sagittarian spirit into a veritable slough of despond. Our buoyant, optimistic Sagittarius is perhaps the sign most prone to depressions which, to the outsider, seem out of all proportion to the disappointment which triggered them. Sagittarians would benefit from the lighter touch of their opposite sign Gemini which favours specific connections over broad generalisations.

THE EARTH SIGNS

Taurus 20 April – 20 May
Arguably the most uncomplicated sign of the zodiac, Taurus provides a container in which the energy symbolised by fiery Aries can sprout. Taurus is a 'yin' or feminine earth sign. Taurus comes at that point in the Sun's annual cycle when the warm, wet earth enables things to grow, slowly and safely. On village greens all over England, ritual fertility rites were enacted at this time in the form of the May Queen and her attendants dancing round the phallic maypole. Ruled by Venus, planet of

beauty and harmony, in Taurus we connect with the natural world and value the beauty of its colours, shapes and forms. Indeed I know many Taureans who have wonderfully green fingers and derive enormous pleasure from making things grow whether in a rose garden, a vegetable patch or in plant pots in a city flat. Taurus' symbol is the cow or bull and both animals have connotations of fertility and nourishment. In Egyptian mythology the cow-headed goddess Hathor was said to have created the world, and statues depict her nourishing the living with her milk. This aspect of Taurus is the archetypal Earth Mother who protects and nourishes all living things.

In essence a supremely physical sign, Taureans are in touch with the body and the senses. They like to feel good and enjoy basic pleasures in eating, sleeping and sex. A colleague at work with Sun in Taurus loved eating biscuits which he said made him feel happy! Taureans never skip lunch and grow miserable if they have to endure periods without food, warmth, affection and home comforts.

Great sensualists, Taureans, or Venus in Taurus in the birth chart, have an unhurried, easy, uncomplicated approach to physical pleasures which are generously given and warmly received. Physically demonstrative, Taureans often have a well-developed sense of touch and love to have their backs rubbed. Emotionally, Taureans form long and strong attachments to partners, home and possessions. It is from the tangible and the physical that Taureans gain their emotional security – long-distance love affairs or agreements in principle are not enough. And once Taureans put down their roots, you will need to dig deep and hard to shift them.

Venus endows Taureans with a love of beauty, like the other Venus-ruled sign Libra. However, Taurus is a practical sign, and likes to translate this urge into acquiring or creating something, from a lovingly made piece of pottery to a comfortable home where textures, shapes, colour and atmosphere combine beautifully. Whatever Taureans turn their hand to, the process is as important as the finished work. Sometimes, however, the process takes so long that you begin to wonder if you will ever see any results! Airy and fiery types find the Taurean pace of life annoyingly slow. Yet when we are feeling stressed or unwell, Taurus' presence is very soothing. Venus also endows Taureans with a certain grace – dancers Margot Fonteyn and Martha Graham have this Sun sign.

The less attractive side of Taurus is their tendency to see only what is in front of their noses, ignoring anything which does not conform to their rather narrow view. They are uncomfortable with the world of fantasy and the imagination, and have a tendency to dismiss films or books which operate on this level as 'rubbish'. A fitting image is the Indian cow or bull which toils up and down, ploughing a deeper and deeper furrow, totally unaware of what is happening anywhere but in its own particular field. So, Taurus, a fixed earth sign, can all too easily get stuck in a rut, obstinately refusing to budge even when the writing is clearly on the wall. The famous Taurean love of the good things in life can also lead to over-indulgence and laziness. Both can give rise to weight problems, as demonstrated by the brilliant, oversize Taurean actor and director Orson Welles who ate and drank to excess. At times Taureans can become greedy and materialistic, finding security through the acquisition of money and possessions. Their need for ownership also extends to people with the result that a Taurean partner or parent may unconsciously view someone close as their 'property'. Taureans hang on for dear life to what they've got or to those views which fit into their scheme of things. This can result in a kind of physical and emotional constipation, an unwillingness to digest what they find unacceptable. Taureans might benefit from a good dose of their opposite number Scorpio's internal spring cleaning skills. It might enable their clogged systems to let go – of old habits, possessions and people.

Virgo 23 August – 22 September

Virgo is a mutable earth sign, traditionally represented by a corn-maiden. Just as all Scorpios are not sexually insatiable, so Virgos are not all as prudish and hygiene-conscious as popular Sun sign astrology would have us believe. In fact Virgo is something of a paradox since the chaste corn-maiden is a variation on the theme of the fertile Earth Mother or Moon goddess. In ancient Egypt and Babylon, the temple priestesses who served the Great Goddess expressed their allegiance through their sexuality. Virgin, in those times, meant belonging to no man and present day Virgos, both male and female, have a definite air of self-containment. Virgo, like the other earth signs, operates very much on a physical, sensual level, and anyone with Sun, Moon, or Ascendant in this sign is very much their own person, forming relationships freely when they choose. Virgo's self-sufficiency may even mean living alone since the process of self-understanding is very important to them. To this sign we assign the archetypal Old Maid or Confirmed Batchelor who are likely to be happy in their ordered existence, however much the rest of society laments their partnerless status.

I feel sure that the person who invented the Filofax must have a strong Virgo streak! Even though Virgos can be sluttish at home or at work, you always get the impression that their minds are as neatly organised as their Filofaxes. Prone to list-making, Virgos like to plan ahead, making sure they are well-prepared and well-briefed. One long-suffering typically Virgoan boss was wont to chide me with the words, 'You mustn't short-cut the system!' Fastidious, correct Virgo never misses a thing, like writer Jane Austen. Her impeccably written books contain acute character observations and extremely detailed descriptions of her social milieu. Virgoan Agatha Christie's plots are meticulously constructed, and her professional sleuths tie up every loose end. Virgo, an earth sign ruled by Mercury, has a practical, discriminating mind with well-developed critical and analytical faculties. Virgo sees expressing criticism as a positive, helpful quality. It often takes the form of self-criticism and Virgos can be very hard on themselves if they fall short of their own particularly high standards. Erring on the side of under-valuing, rather than over-valuing, their achievements, Virgo strives for the perfection the more confident signs like Leo think they have already achieved. The impeccable Sir Laurence Olivier has his Moon in Virgo.

Virgo is said to rule the intestines and the sixth house which has to do with health. Indeed, the Virgoan mind likes to digest information, breaking it down and sifting out what is useful. Yet the Virgoan personality is aware that the mind cannot be separated from the body and many Virgos are health conscious, and especially interested in diet and nutrition. Also on a physical level many Virgos are skilled with their hands. The Virgo corn-maiden symbol signifies fruitfulness and creativity. Whereas the Taurean or Libran might be more concerned with the look or the feel of their work, Virgo concentrates on fine craftsmanship and the finished product will be well designed.

When the Virgo critical faculty is unleashed it can often manifest in hair-splitting of the worst kind. Discussions degenerate into arguments if you don't use the right word or, heaven forbid, say something which contradicts what you said earlier. And Virgos can be merciless if they think your work isn't up to scratch or your behaviour isn't all it should be. Their over-concern with getting things right, which includes you, often manifests in hurtful and unconstructive criticism. If you want to know whether you look nice in your new outfit, don't be surprised if your Virgo partner only notices that the hem isn't straight! Virgo can be very long-sighted when it comes to the simple or the obvious. They will spend months decorating the bathroom or sanding a cupboard, so absorbed in the process that they forget other people need to actually use things. This rather immaculate side of Virgos is a manifestation of the need to be effective and in control of their environment. Virgos fear chaos and disorder and can become anxious and stressed if everything isn't going according to plan. Under pressure, the mental side of Virgo refuses to switch off and nervous complaints such as insomnia and indigestion can develop. If Virgos could learn to relax a little and go with the flow like their opposite sign, Pisces, they might find that things that happen spontaneously are often all the more enjoyable for it.

Capricorn 22 December – 19 January

Capricorn is a cardinal earth sign whose symbol is a goat with a fishy tail. Given this sign's reputation for social achievement, it is almost as if the symbol refers to the ambitious fish sub-personality of our Capricorn who much prefers to be climbing up mountains than swimming around in a big pond at the bottom. Mythical goat figures such as the Greek god Pan also throw some light on the nature of Capricorn. Pan with his horns and hoofs personifies the fertile spirit of nature. Often depicted chasing nymphs, he expresses a lecherous delight in pleasures of the senses. Capricorn is a cardinal earth sign with a definitely 'horny', playful side. However, this is usually obscured by a rather straight-laced, sensible exterior since Capricorn is ruled by Saturn, stern father and teacher of difficult lessons. Capricorns aren't often to be found crawling round the floor wearing silly hats at Christmas parties. They have their reputations to think of!

Capricorn is associated with the Father, and by extension with authority figures in general. Stalin, Nixon, and Mao Tse Tung were all born when the Sun was in Capricorn. Capricorns, more than any other sign, seem to have problems with authority. Much preferring to be in control themselves, many Capricorns are happier being their own boss, working for themselves on a self-employed basis. One Capricornian man even admitted to being unemployable! Capricorns are notoriously economical and it is not unusual to find them drawing up budgets and controlling the purse strings, both professionally and at home. Capricorns like to build things, from shelves and houses to their own businesses. One Capricornian friend has his own building company. Liking responsibility and willing to work hard to gain experience, Capricorns are not afraid of long-term commitment. They exude a solidity and dependability which makes them seem indispensable at work, and trustworthy and enduring in friendships. This Capricornian durability is based on good solid experience. Capricorns have little time for abstract arguments not based on personal experience, especially their own. This explains the sign's liking for the traditional which has stood the test of time.

Capricorns age well, like good wine or classically proportioned architecture. Capricorn singer and musician David Bowie has retained his popularity since the 1960s. Often they seem to have been born wise and with an innate understanding of the rules. As in the game of cricket, Capricorns have an early awareness of regulations and boundaries. This mature outlook may mean that Capricornian children seem more like adults. At least they don't get accused of having no respect for the older generation! Often Capricorn is the one trusted with responsibility in the family, or early in their careers. Strongly Capricornian types soon learn that right behaviour and doing one's duty reap rewards in life. They wisely follow the beaten track, wary of the short cut which may turnout to be a dead end. Enduring Capricorns often choose difficult paths which require discipline and dedication, such as spiritual growth, or practices which require physical and mental control such as yoga. Famous spiritual teachers Krishnamurti and Gurdjieff were born when the Sun was in Capricorn.

It will come as no surprise to learn that all that Capricornian hard work, responsibility and discipline leaves very little time for having fun. Capricorns don't play easily – they're too busy acting grown up. Unfortunately this can result in many Capricorns refusing to take off their hair shirts or laying aside their heavy crosses. 'Life is hard, then you die' is a philosophy dear to the Capricorn heart. An amusing phrase but ultimately depressing – and depression is something many Capricorns come to experience. What can bring a little lightness into Capricorns' lives, ironically, lies within them. Getting in touch with the playful, inner child, through their own children, other people's or working with children, can dispel the Capricornian gloom. Capricorn also has much to learn from the trusting nature and uninhibited expression of children. Capricorn is said to be associated with the bones, and especially the knees. Many people with a strong emphasis on this sign are afraid of looking a fool, or having to get down on their knees. Here Capricorn might look to the opposite side of Cancer which can be emotionally vulnerable and admits to feelings of dependency on others.

THE AIR SIGNS

Gemini 21 May – 20 June

Gemini is a mutable air sign. Its symbol, the twins, shows the essentially dualistic nature of the sign. The story of the famous mythological twins, Castor and Pollux, born of the same mother but with two different fathers, one mortal and one immortal, illustrates the two sides of Gemini. When Castor died in battle, the two were re-united, albeit for brief periods, when they made a kind of cosmic time-share deal with Zeus. This enabled them to alternate periods in the mortal world with the realm of the gods. They met at changeover time. Cain and Abel embody the dark and light aspects of the sign. When Cain kills his brother, he carries a mark which serves as a reminder of his deed. Super-rational Gemini too is often aware of his or her irrational alter ego which often surfaces in the form of negative thoughts or unruly emotions. Ruled by Mercury, swift moving planet of communication, Gemini likes to analyse, classify and relate one thing to another in order to make sense of reality. Acutely observant and with a gift for making connections, the speedy Gemini intellect loves to be presented with a problem to be untangled, sorted out and communicated. You can almost see the light bulb flash on over their heads as the pieces fit together. Arthur Conan Doyle, creator of one of the great fictional mystery solvers, Sherlock Holmes, was a Sun Gemini.

Geminis, like the other air signs, need room to manoeuvre. Resistant to any kind of timetabling of their movements, if you ask them what they will be doing on Thursday evening they are likely to look uncomfortable and say 'Why do you want to know?' Notoriously difficult to pin down Gemini flits, butterfly-like, from one flower to the next or from one group of people to the next. Socially adroit, unless Saturn is around in the chart to put a damper on things, our Gemini can be talkative, witty, amusing, and light as air. The playful Gemini mind can often be infuriatingly clever. When involved with a strongly Geminian type in a discussion or a debate, you often find that you have unfortunately contradicted yourself three times or tied yourself up in verbal knots. Or a Gemini may even begin to mimic someone's accent or gestures – delightful, as long as they aren't yours and you are out of earshot!

Geminis, however, are not essentially malicious, like children they just love to play. Watch out for that wicked gleam in their eye as they play devil's advocate in a discussion or meeting they have become bored with. And they get bored easily, especially if people around them can't keep up with the energetic pace at which they operate mentally, and sometimes physically. Geminis like to be on the move and in touch with what is happening in the outside world, reading the newspaper and watching or listening to the news are important to Geminis. If the car won't start, or the telephone is out of order, you will witness a distinctly uncomfortable Gemini. They like openings and usually leave themselves a loophole or two so they can exit if the going gets rough or they have lost interest. Indeed, they are also quick to spot an opening, and it is a rare Gemini who doesn't like making deals of one sort or another. Hermes (Mercury, ruler of Gemini) was, after all, the god of traders and entrepreneurs. Robert Maxwell, a Sun Gemini, combines this sign's entrepreneurial qualities with a gift for communication – on an international scale.

The shady side of Gemini is not so light and airy. Hermes was also the god of thieves and liars. Gemini can at times be very economical with the truth. You won't be told huge whoppers, but the words or the situation will have been arranged in such a way as to be open to maximum interpretation. Gemini can be a very tricky customer, so make sure you have your wits about you too. Like freewheeling Sagittarius, Geminis are terrified of being pinned down. They have a horror of commitment but, as you would expect with such a dualistic sign, they have double standards. Other people are expected to commit themselves first. Impish and eternally youthful, Geminis often have more than just a passing resemblance to Peter Pan, the boy who didn't want to grow up. Gemini Paul McCartney still manages to look like a cheeky schoolboy. Poet and musician, Bob Dylan, gives his Gemini Sun sign away in songs such as 'Forever Young', while Gemini actress Joan Collins never seems to look any older. Gemini spends a great deal of time resisting the ageing process. But youth, vigour and beauty do not last, however fanatical Geminis may be about their looks. When responsibility or age catches up with them. Gemini can turn into the sort of depressed, 'heavy' person he or she is so desperate to avoid. Rather than stay in the surface world of appearances and small talk, Gemini might usefully learn a thing or two about the deeper and wider issues of life from opposite number, Sagittarius.

Libra 23 September – 22 October
Libra is a cardinal air sign, ruled by Venus, planet of relating, beauty and harmony. In the Egyptian goddess Maat who weighed the hearts of the dead on her scales, we have a lovely image for this, the sign of balance. Maat herself, or her symbol, a feather, sat on one side of the scales and if the heart on the other was not heavy but in

perfect equilibrium, the soul passed into a happy eternity. Librans on the whole rarely achieve a state of balance, although they constantly seek the middle way. Their lives are often bedevilled by choice. One Libran client said it was a daily problem, while another, with Libra rising, went some way towards a solution to the problem of being faced with two alternatives by choosing neither and instead taking up a third option! Librans, as you might expect with a planetary ruler like Venus, are often incurable romantics, and of course in their ideal world, all would be peace, love, beauty and harmony. Often, Librans achieve external balance. Colours are tasteful and co-ordinated, and atmospheres are harmonious since tactful, diplomatic Librans make perfect hosts and hostesses. Other people and their reactions are very important to Libra which is the half-way point of the zodiacal wheel. At this point we become conscious of the needs of others in society and the value of social interaction.

Perhaps the most ethical sign of the zodiac, ultra-reasonable Librans like to play fair and see justice done. Libran Bob Geldof saw the unfairness and injustice inherent in a world where some consumed to excess while others starved, and launched Band Aid. They often have a kind of *quid pro quo* approach to life which means that they tend to ask a favour of someone if and when their account with that person, metaphorically speaking, is in credit. In fact Librans are often good with money since they are motivated to balance the books! Libran Margaret Thatcher's dictum is 'a fair day's work for a fair day's pay'. Fair also means attractive or beautiful and Librans are very susceptible to nice-looking things and nice-looking people. Often to be found in the fields of literature and the visual arts, Librans are drawn to culture and usually have a strongly developed aesthetic sense. They like to behave in a civilised manner, finding more earthy types rather offensive. One artist friend with Libra rising was heard to exclaim that women were 'so civilised' (compared to brute men!).

It is, however, a mistake to see Librans as pushovers.

The cardinal signs like to be initiators and one apposite description of Libra is 'a polite Aries'. Librans listen intently to your point of view and give much consideration to your opinions. Then, like skilled diplomats and persuasive sales people, they flatter you and secure your agreement and co-operation. Librans are wonderful at playing office politics or any other kind of politics because, like the other air signs they like to reason and mediate. Pacifists at heart, they try to redress the balance between co-operation and conflict. (I have my Moon in Libra and at the moment I am helping to research and edit a book on World Peace!) Even those with the assertive planet Mars in Libra seem to find a suitably graceful outlet for their energy. One male client went to dance classes in his spare time. The 'gentler' martial arts like T'ai Chi would be equally appropriate.

So where do we experience the not-so-nice side of Libra? Librans can be arty, they can also be crafty. Cardinal signs are goal-orientated and sweet-talking Librans usually manage to get what they want by being everybody's friend. To other, more direct types, however, the Libran courtesy can appear downright smarmy and eminently untrustworthy. Librans need to be liked and sometimes that can manifest in emotional dishonesty – always telling people what they want to hear. Putting things tactfully is a Libran forte, but many people with this sign strongly emphasised are amazed when others react with anger and hostility. How a remark is couched does not necessarily alter its content, and however nice the Libran manner, confrontational or highly personal statements will inevitably provoke others to react defensively. Librans, in short, are prone to repress anger and unfortunately, when it inevitably surfaces, it may appear in the form of brutally honest and insensitive remarks, or illness. Seeing all sides of an issue can result in chronic indecision, and many Librans become paralysed in the face of choice. But perhaps finding themselves constantly in positions where they have to make a choice is the only way to get Librans down from their fences. Life is not always fair or pleasant and Librans can learn from their opposite sign, Aries, the value of self-assertion so they can express themselves with more directness and honesty.

Aquarius 20 January – 18 February

Aquarius is a fixed air sign and yet its symbol is the water bearer. This may seems confusing but if we focus on the clarity and freshness of the water the meaning of the sign begins to reveal itself. Aquarius is like a new broom, sweeping away the traditional ways of thinking and established forms of behaviour as laid down by the preceding sign, Capricorn. Without the broad Aquarian view, the progressive and the alternative would never find their way into society. So, Aquarius represents thought and ideas, for it is an air sign, which are based on a vision of the future. Far-seeing Aquarius lives in the world of tomorrow, eager to embrace new forms of technology and excited by alternative viewpoints. Uranus, the planetary ruler of Aquarius, was a remote god of the highest heavens. From his lofty satellite-like perch, he could observe the whole of life on earth as it unfolded beneath him. This breadth of vision is one of the strongest characteristics of the Aquarian personality who is tolerant, open-minded and watchful of humanity. The structuring planet Saturn also rules Aquarius – once a new idea or viewpoint has been accepted, it is absorbed into the mainstream and becomes a convention, making way for the next fresh approach.

The Aquarian temperament is scientific, truth-seeking and egalitarian in outlook. Concerned with accessibility, sharing and companionship Aquarius is the tireless social reformer who campaigns for equal rights in the welfare state. In the sign of Aquarius we enlarge the one-to-one Libran view of relationships to encompass people as a whole. Aquarius has a definite social conscience. This means that Aquarians are more concerned with issues that affect all of us together, rather than at an individual or personal level. Like the other air signs, Aquarius likes freedom of movement and, particularly, of expression. The notions of free speech, freedom of information and human rights are all dear to Aquarian hearts. It is interesting that as we move into the Age of Aquarius censorship and freedom are topical subjects. The British Government was unable to ban the publication of *Spycatcher*, while Aquarian US President Reagan has focused on the human rights issue in summit meetings with Mr Gorbachev. The Soviet Union seems to be opening her doors in a spirit of co-operation and greater freedom of expression.

Uranus, the awakening planet, likes to jolt us out of our sleep, and a characteristic of the strongly Aquarian person is the desire to shock. This can take the form of attacking safe, traditional views, the establishment and orthodoxy in general. Aquarians are iconoclasts and individualists without match. Two famous examples are Germaine Greer and Virginia Woolf. Germaine Greer outraged public opinion by her frank, outspoken views on female sexuality. Virginia Woolf's individuality was reflected in opinions and ideas about women incompatible with her times, as well as in her unusual literary style. James Dean was another Aquarian who typified the sign's spirit of youthful rebellion. It is important for Aquarians that people recognise their freedom as individuals. However, if you try to impose your views on the Aquarian personality, you may be surprised to discover a wilful streak in our tolerant, humanitarian Aquarian who is prone to rebel by perversely and doggedly expressing the view which is most opposite to yours. Remember, Aquarius is a fixed air sign and also under the influence of the controlling planet Saturn which, taken together, can result in distinctly unliberal, dogmatic attitudes of the 'you're free to express your opinion as long as it agrees with mine' variety. Strongly individualistic Aquarians also tend to dominate people of a more sensitive disposition. Aquarians are unhappy with feelings and displays of emotion which they see as sticky messes best avoided. They love people, but find great difficulty relating on a person-to-person basis.

In close relationships Aquarians find it difficult to make any compromises where their independence is concerned. This can be hurtful for those who need commitment and intimacy. In this respect Aquarians might look to their opposite sign, Leo, for a much warmer way of relating whilst still acknowledging the need to be treated as a person in one's own right.

THE WATER SIGNS

Cancer 21 June – 22 July

Cancer is a cardinal water sign and its symbol is the crab. Crabs live both on land and in the water and Cancers are at home both in the real world and in the shifting seas of the imagination. They don't tackle issues head on but go about their business in a roundabout way which resembles the sideways scurrying of the crab. Watery Cancer is very much a feeling sign. When difficult emotions like fear or sorrow filter through their scaly armour to the soft fleshy centre, Cancers scuttle rapidly back to their holes to reflect. At such times Cancerian types need to find a bigger or harder shell to contain them in their vulnerability, rather like hermit crabs. While waiting for this new covering Cancers lie awake, fearful of the approach of scavenging seagulls in search of prey.

Cancers need a home, a nest, which is a source of comfort and security, and also a place of retreat like the crab's shell. Ruled by the ever-changing Moon, Cancerian moods fluctuate like the tides. One Cancerian man lives in a shell-like houseboat on a tidal river, sometimes stationary on the muddy bank, sometimes gently rocking in the water. The Moon, Cancer's ruling planet, is a symbol of the Mother, and has associations with containers and feeling contained. Cancers need the kind of emotional security which ideally we felt in childhood. especially from whichever of our parents we experienced as the most maternal. This security, for Cancers, is a necessary barrier against the intrusion of outsiders into the inner world of the sometimes fearful, vulnerable and hypersensitive child who lives behind the shell-like facade. Cancers' brittle self-protectiveness masks a deep anxiety that they might be humiliated or lose face. Yet, like the new Moon or a theatre in temporary financial straights, they always reappear after going dark for a while. Don't take this personally. Cancers like a good sulk occasionally, even if it lasts for a week.

Like the elephant, Cancers never forget, or if they do it takes them a very long time indeed. They like to hoard objects which have a sentimental value to nourish their soft-centres. Cancers in fact can be very sentimental, liking nothing better than fond reminiscences about the good old days. Indeed it is important for the strongly Cancerian person to be in touch with their roots. They like to feel part of a continuity, to be in touch with where they came from in terms of family, community, country and culture. Many Cancers can remember their childhoods vividly, like writer Marcel Proust, famous for the bitter-sweet nostalgia of his *Memories of Things Past* or Laurie Lee whose popular *Cider with Rosie* described his happy early years in Gloucestershire. Highly imaginative, the Cancerian memory is a deep well of rich material on which to draw.

I have noticed a 'maternal', nurturing side in Cancers regardless of sex. It may be easy for women to express this traditionally female quality through motherhood. However, many Cancerian people find their way into the helping professions and make natural counsellors and therapists. Another way in which Cancers express their caring side is through feeding other people, not to mention themselves. For Cancers, food is not merely fuel to keep us alive, it is a form of indispensable inner nourishment. Cancers need to feed their emotions and imagination, as well as their bodies. With the uncanny intuitive ability of the water signs, they instinctively know when others need feeding too. Cancers read other peoples' emotional undercurrents like other people read books. Iris Murdoch is another Cancerian writer who skilfully conveys the complex inner life of her characters.

Cancers' strength is also paradoxically their weakness –
they need to be needed. This, however, does not go down
very well with the more airy types who need breathing
space. Once the Cancerian pincers have made emotional
contact, they hardly ever relax their hold. Possessive to a
fault, Cancers often alienate those they love by playing all
sorts of emotional games to get their own way. Once they
understand your own emotional sore spots, they are not
above putting the pincer in. Sadly, this often leads to
rejection. An unhappy Cancer can be emotionally
childlike, desperately clingy and moody, and defensive at
the merest hint of criticism. Warmth and support can turn
to touchiness and bitchiness as we see the Old Womanish
side of Cancer which delights in talking about other
peoples' misfortunes. Since Cancer rules the stomach,
emotional upsets can lead to indigestion. Cancers could
learn from their opposite sign Capricorn the value of
self-motivation as opposed to living through others.
Cancers' natural sympathy and responsiveness can be
used creatively for their own benefit when they put
themselves first.

Scorpio 23 October – 21 November

Scorpio is a fixed water sign and its symbol is the scorpion.
Scorpions, as you would expect, figure more strongly in the
mythologies of countries like Egypt which have large
tracts of desert. Selket, the scorpion goddess, protected
the Egyptian dead and played an active part in the
embalming process, guarding the jar which contained the
intestines. Scorpio, then, is associated with death and
rebirth, but also with purification and elimination
processes like the function of the colon. Both the eagle and
the phoenix are associated with the sign. Legend has it
that eagles renew their plumage by flying up to the sun,
then plunging down into the sea – the phoenix is reborn
from the ashes. Scorpios, ruled by Mars and Pluto, can
both soar to great heights and plumb the depths. They are
not interested in half measures. Scorpions hunt their prey

at night and strongly Scorpionic types are not afraid to confront the darker side of their own and other people's natures. With an uncanny instinct for perceiving hidden motives, such as power, sex or money, Scorpios recognise the contradictions inherent in all of us and soon lose their innocence.

Scorpio has been called the sign of absolute self-mastery. Both planetary rulers, Mars and Pluto, denote strength of will and determination. Once Scorpios have embarked on their chosen path, the mind, the body and the emotions are all subjected to the kind of stringent control practised by an SAS officer or a Zen master! Still waters run deep and although there may be strong currents beneath the surface, self-disciplined Scorpios present to the world an exterior so impassive as to appear almost mask-like. Disciplines like the martial arts and yoga often attract Scorpios not only because they require strength and stillness, but also because their underlying philosophies are essentially mystical or spiritual.

Scorpio is indeed a sign with a strong mystical dimension and this is perhaps most apparent in their attitude to sex. Allegedly obsessed with copulation, male Scorpios are supposed to be Casanovas while the females are reputed to have a deadly siren-like quality, luring poor unfortunate men onto the rocks. Although many Scorpios do possess a kind of sexual magnetism, they are acutely aware of the mystical dimension of sex and its potentially healing quality. In fact Scorpios are eminently capable of a spartan denial of their sexuality altogether once the magic has disappeared.

Scorpio is a fixed water sign and feels things intensely. Often such emotions are difficult to put into words and then Scorpios keep silent and appear brooding. Fearful of being misunderstood and alienating others by seeming too 'heavy', Scorpio has acquired the reputation of the most secretive sign of the zodiac. Like the pent-up power of a dam, Scorpios can use their emotional intensity to help others with their own self-development. Most Scorpios usually get stung quite early on in life. They understand pain and are often drawn to the healing professions, whether as doctors, surgeons or psychotherapists. Sigmund Freud had Scorpio rising while Prince Charles, a Sun Scorpio, championed the cause of alternative medicine and revealed a secret wish to be a healer. When Scorpios do put their feelings into words, the results may not make for light reading, but they are not easily forgotten. Famous Scorpio poets include Dylan Thomas, Sylvia Plath, John Keats and Thomas Chatterton. In all their personal lives we see evidence of the creative and destructive stamp of Scorpio, the heights and the depths.

Scorpio's negative traits may seem more extreme because they are characterised by an intensity of feeling. Scorpio's inner many-headed monster can emerge as resentment, jealousy, violence, revenge, or any form of obsession. If Scorpios hold on to these primitive urges, or they remain hidden, the pressure becomes too great and then we get the full force of the scorpion's deadly sting. Scorpio gossip columnist Nigel Dempster and satirist Auberon Waugh make a living from it! And Scorpios, because they have an intuitive understanding of the uncivilised aspects of human beings, aim below the belt, especially when their own survival is threatened. Rather than submit to someone else's power, many Scorpios will do a self-destruct, like real scorpions, and sting themselves to death. Magnetic Scorpio actress Viven Leigh remarked 'My birth sign is Scorpio and they eat themselves up and burn themselves out.' Power and the abuse of power are Scorpio themes. Scorpios become masters and mistresses by devious routes, quietly but relentlessly getting their own way. And Scorpios are not above creating dreadful scenes just to get a reaction. For Scorpios it is perhaps better to feel terrible than to feel nothing. Taurus, Scorpio's opposite sign, teaches the value of stability and the pleasure to be gained from things simple, rather than extreme. Scorpios could learn from Taurus to be less probing and let things be – some doors are better left unopened.

Pisces 19 February – 20 March

Pisces is a mutable water sign and its symbol is two fishes tied together but swimming in opposite directions. Fish symbolism has been around for a long time, indeed, fish were the emblem of the early Christian Church. Christ chose his disciples from amongst fishermen, who were also 'fishers of men', and the story of his division of the loaves and fishes to feed the multitude is well known. Salmon were sacred to the Celts. So, fish have a kind of other worldly connection and a religious significance. Although not all Pisceans are religious by definition many possess the qualities of compassion, self-sacrifice, forgiveness and humility, which we would associate with religious or spiritual conviction. People in need of help turn to empathetic Pisceans for sympathy and understanding. When Pisceans say they 'know exactly how you feel' they do, and they mean it. One client with a demanding full-time job still found time for voluntary work as a Samaritan. She had her Moon in Pisces. Buddhism is a philosophy with which many Pisceans can identify since it teaches learning through suffering and the way of non-attachment. Pisceans are not reknowned for their worldly or materialistic natures. What is theirs is also yours.

The fluid underwater world of the Piscean fish is characterised by shifting emotional currents and changing colours. Shafts of light penetrate the surface and illuminate the Piscean imagination. Pisces is a sign of poets, like French symbolist Mallarme or American Robert Lowell, and writers such as Lawrence Durrell whose work has a poetic, mythical dimension. Since Neptune, Pisces' planetary ruler, is a planet of illusion, many Piscean types are to be found in the world of the theatre, cinema and photography. Piscean actors and actresses have the uncanny ability to actually become the character they are playing, like chameleons. Indeed, Pisces is said to contain a little bit of each of the other signs. The line between fact and fiction, reality and illusion, is rather more blurred for Pisceans, who long to escape the pain of harsh reality. They take refuge in Hollywood movies, TV soap operas, or Chopin (another Pisces) piano concertos, depending on your taste! This Piscean longing for another soft-focus world is one interpretation of the symbol of the twin fish swimming in opposite directions. Pisces is the last sign of the zodiac wheel. The fish both look forward to a rebirth in the sign of Aries, yet at the same time look back wistfully to where they came from. Illusion in whatever form provides a necessary anaesthetic to dull the pain of harsh reality.

Pisces has the natural intuitive ability of the water signs to tune in to the emotional undertow. Prone to blotting up atmospheres, the Pisces psychic thermometer gauges the emotional temperature in the room. Pisces will rejoice with you but also share your lows. Pisceans can be acutely responsive to the moods and needs of their partners. Often drawn into problematic relationships, romantic Pisces genuinely believes that love conquers all. Sacrificing one's needs or aspirations is a common theme in Piscean involvements. Pisces is associated with the twelfth house of the chart which traditionally has affiliations with seclusion and places of healing or retreat. Pisceans may eschew relationships, choosing to devote their time to helping and healing others. And some part of the Piscean character will always be hidden and just as you catch a glimpse, it slips through your fingers. Pisceans can be very private people and need space and time for their inner feelings and dreams.

Pisces is a mutable sign and its twin fishes cannot agree on which direction to take. Prone to vacillation and inaction when faced with making decisions or moves, Pisceans run the risk of drifting along aimlessly. Yet Pisceans often mask their inner confusion by paying more attention to detail than Virgo. One bureaucratic Piscean colleague threatened to drown everyone in a flood of office memos. At home the spirit which moves Pisces may be the sort that you buy from the off-licence. Pisces' yearning for something higher or greater than themselves is virtually impossible to fulfil in the real world. Piscean Elizabeth

Taylor found an escape route in alcohol and drugs. In relationships too we see this longing for total merging. Unfortunately, Pisces' partner often has a healthy awareness of boundaries and retreats, fearful of being swallowed whole. On the other hand Pisceans don't tend to discriminate, which can be hurtful if you thought you held a special place in their hearts. Pisces can be all things to all people. Deception and self-deception are some of the less appealing traits of this slippery sign. Pisceans might benefit from the down-to-earth discrimination of their opposite, Virgo, and make a clearer distinction between fantasy and reality.

6.
ASTROLOGY AND THE FAMILY

THE FAMILY INHERITANCE

The family is a living organism. We draw up a family 'tree' when we want to know more about previous generations and, like a tree, the family has ancestral roots which extend deep below the surface. They form the foundation for future generations and nourish new growth. As individuals we are part of this complex system of roots, branches, and leaves which stretch down to the past and upwards and outwards to the future. Blood, as the saying goes, is thicker than water. There are few ties forged of stronger material than those between blood relatives. By means of such ties the family tree is able to flourish and bear fruit. Certain branches may wither and fall off, but their nutrients are reabsorbed into the earth surrounding the base of the tree. Most societies rely heavily on the stabilising effect of the family. The family unit helps us to feel rooted in society – it gives us a sense of belonging.

However, divorce in the UK is now twenty times more common than it was fifty years ago, affecting one in three marriages. A recent newspaper article (June 1988) estimates that the number of children in the UK now living in some sort of step-family is as high as 50 per cent. In marriages where stepchildren are involved the divorce rate is higher, at one in two. Almost all the children interviewed in this article experienced massive upheavals when their parents split up. Some of the younger children secretly hoped that their natural parents would one day be reunited. Some of the older children felt they no longer had a place where they belonged and could only discuss their problems with other stepchildren, not parents or step-parents. Some understandably, asserted that they would never get married. Slowly but surely, the health of the family tree is beginning to deteriorate. You could even say that the family tree was in danger of being felled.

As in Darwin's theory of evolution, only the strongest and fittest of families seem to be surviving intact. These are, for the most part, the kinds of 'enmeshed' families where there is close and continuous communication. Family members may prefer to make their homes in the same town or region of the country. There may even be a family business, profession, or trade which enables certain children to follow in their parents' footsteps. However, not everyone in this close-knit family community may wish to tread the appointed path. A particular individual may feel temperamentally unsuited to carry on the family tradition. Then what happens? The family is quite capable of closing ranks and making it very difficult for the individual to express his individuality. One client, the son of a highly successful businessman, rejected his father's materialism and chose to go to art college. A

sensitive Sun in Cancer, he hid behind a witty and
amusing Gemini Ascendant, taking on the role of court
jester to the family. His family, however, were totally
unaware of the sadness and confusion behind the jolly
mask. His role fitted nicely into the family scenario, so
no-one ever asked about his personal life, or even, simply,
whether he was really happy. In fact, he had been gay for
some years but felt unable to admit it openly. Involvement
in a destructive relationship was wearing away at his
self-confidence and the stiff drink before work became a
habit.

At the other extreme there are families with very little
apparent cohesion. One son or daughter may have settled
in another region or country and maintain minimal
contact with parents and relatives. Individuals in such
families may seem very different temperamentally. There
is not so much pressure for them to conform since the
family may have no discernible image. One female client
who had left the country of her birth to settle in Britain
described her family as a 'bunch of eccentrics' and was
happy to be allowed to do her own thing. However, such
families offer little in the way of support which can damage
our sense of belonging. One male friend has the Sun
in Cancer in the fourth house, making a difficult aspect to
Neptune. The fourth house is naturally ruled by the Moon
and the sign Cancer and it describes our sense of home
and belonging, our roots, our ethnic and cultural
characteristics. With Neptune cloaking my friend's
fourth-house Sun in a thick fog, his roots seemed to him to
be confused and elusive. In fact, his parents moved abroad
when he was very young. The marriage broke down, and
both parents now live abroad separately in different
countries. My friend, although born and still residing in
Britain, does not really feel British. The theme of getting
in touch with roots and origins runs through all his
creative work. Most of us feel a need to belong somewhere
and carry within us those family blood ties in the same
way that we bear a facial similarity to other family
members. The connections are there even if we choose to

put a few thousand miles between ourselves and our parents.

FAMILY PATTERNS IN THE CHART

When I drew up the charts of my own family, including grandparents, I was amazed at the similarity. Certain signs and aspects cropped up with alarming regularity, running through the family like a physical likeness, whether it be blonde hair and blue eyes or red hair and freckles. Out of a family of four children, two are Sun Scorpio, one Sun Aquarius, the other Sun Libra. My parents are both Sun Scorpio, one has the Moon in Aquarius, the other the Moon in Libra. Two of us have Aquarius rising, the other two have Libra. Both grandmothers and three aunts have the Sun in Aquarius. Even the element balance between fire, earth, air and water signs follows the same pattern. Both my parents lack planets in the earth signs, and we four children only managed to come up with four planets in earth signs between us – out of a total of 40 planets! In another family the father has his Sun in Gemini while the mother has her Moon in Gemini. One of the two sons is a Sun Gemini, while the other has the Moon in Gemini. One of yet another father's two daughters has the Moon in the same sign as his, Aquarius. The other has her Moon in Gemini, the sign on his Ascendant. Out of a total of 30 degrees, the Moon of one of the daughter's I have just mentioned happens to be in the same degree as her father's. When you realise that the Moon takes just under a month to travel through all twelve signs, and moves one degree every two hours, the chances of a parent's Moon being in the same sign, let alone the same degree, as a child's are, statistically speaking, very slim indeed.

The pattern woven by astrology through the family is very striking, but it should not surprise us too much. After all, we are the product of our parents, and our grandparents before them. We share likenesses of both a physical and temperamental nature. It seems only natural that the birth chart should reflect these inherited similarities. On a physiological and psychological level it can be likened to the genetic code which is stored in the double helix of DNA, the principal constituent of chromosomes, the structures which transmit hereditary characteristics. At some point in our lives we have all heard that most familiar of exclamations, 'Oh! you're just like your mother' or 'you're just like your father', especially when we demonstrate one of their more annoying characteristics. Such likenesses appear in the birth chart in the form of inherited signs and aspects. One female friend, known to be energetic and assertive, has Mars strongly placed in Aries in her chart. When I drew up the charts of her two daughters, born two years apart, I found that both of them also had Mars in Aries. No wonder she remarked that they both got very upset if they didn't get their own way!

However, no two charts are alike, and while there are similarities and patterns in family charts, there will also be variations. No single child is going to inherit all the mother's or all the father's characteristics, neither will these characteristics be divided equally among the children. Family traits do not conform to precise mathematical formulae. Each person is an individual in his or her own right, born at a given point in space and time. The chart, with its signs, planets and aspects, is a symbolic representation of that unique point or moment. As we grow, our charts unfold it and our lives reflect it.

FINDING THE PARENTS IN THE CHART

Our individual horoscope shows how we react to life and process experience. Children from the same family, the same parents, the same background, can and do react differently. An analysis of the birth chart helps us to understand why we react in a particular way towards our parents. Often, for example, each child experiences the parents in a different way. In one family who I will call the Smiths, two brothers and a sister each had a very different perspective on their father. The elder brother experienced his father as warm, generous and supportive. His sister felt her father had been so distant and uninterested in her that she could barely stand to be in the same room as him. The younger brother, however, felt his father was ineffectual, and that it was his mother who 'wore the trousers'.

Celebrated seventeenth-century astrologer, William Lilly, maintained that planets and their aspects in the tenth house of the birth chart, and/or the sign on the Midheaven, described the Mother. Planets in the fourth house and their aspects, and/or the sign opposite the Midheaven (known as the IC), described the father. Today, the excellent work of Liz Greene bears this out. In my own experience there have been exceptions to this rule, although it seems to apply in the majority of cases. The tenth house describes our image of the society in which we live and our world view. It can be argued that from the child's perspective, our Mother is our first contact with the world 'out there' and our early experiences of mothering shape our attitude to society. For example, a male client with Venus prominent on the Midheaven felt his mother had been loving and supportive. He had an essentially positive and trusting attitude towards life.

The father, on the other hand, is usually a less obvious presence to the child especially if he is out at work all day. Also, in keeping with the planetary ruler of the fourth house, the Moon, which describes where we came from, it is our father's family name that we take as our surname and the chromosome of his cell which decides the sex of a child. A female client with Pluto on the IC said she remembered her father as a powerful, charismatic figure. In keeping with Pluto's mythical attributes as the god of death, her father was almost killed in an accident just before she was born.

Equally important in assessing our experience of our parents in the birth chart are the sign, house, and aspects to the Sun and the Moon. The Sun generally describes our experience of the father, unless the mother was the dominant figure in the marriage in which case she might be represented by the Sun. The Moon, by sign, house, and aspect, describes our experience of the Mother, unless the father related to us in a more 'maternal' manner.

Astrology confirms the dynamics of the Smith family referred to above, where the children experience their parents in different ways. The eldest son's chart shows a lovely aspect between the Sun, Venus and Jupiter – indicating an easy relationship with the father. The sister's chart shows a hard aspect between the Sun and Uranus, indicating tension and a feeling of being disconnected from the father. The younger brother's chart reveals Saturn making a difficult aspect to the Sun – often disappointment with the father – while the Moon conjuncts Pluto, indicating a powerful maternal influence.

TAKING RESPONSIBILITY

What cannot be emphasised too strongly in an astrological analysis of our parents is that the chart shows how we, as individuals, experience them. Other people or society in general may not experience them in a similar fashion. Viewed astrologically, our inner parental image does seem to tally with the outer reality of our parents, as we experience them. No-one has yet come up with a satisfactory explanation as to why the parental image shown in our charts at the moment of birth holds true as we grow older. I am not sure that this can be explained except on a psychological level. Perhaps we get the parents that not only fit the chart, but who are necessary for our own development as individuals. And it is almost as if we are primed to tune in or select those times which correspond best with our particular view of a parent. One astrologer put it very well when she said that a child with the Moon making an easy aspect to generous Jupiter will see a bottle as half full, while a child with Moon aspecting limiting Saturn will choose to see it as half empty! The astrological indicators, whether they show comfortable or uncomfortable parental relationships, appear in our own charts. They may also have appeared in one or other of our parents' charts. However, we must take responsibility for our own lives. Blaming our parents for everything that goes wrong is a singularly futile exercise and a neat way of avoiding looking at our less attractive characteristics.

If, as in the previous example, our chart shows a difficult aspect to the Moon from Saturn we might have experienced our mother as cold, undemonstrative and restricting. We may, as a child, have felt our needs were not met. If no attempt is made to resolve the situation between parent and child, especially while the parent in question is still alive, then a vicious circle ensues. As we grow older, we learn not to expect love and simply stop reaching out. By choosing to behave in this way we ourselves appear cold and unfeeling with the result that people continue to reject us. So the pattern repeats itself and will inevitably affect our relationship with our own children.

A sensitive male friend with the Sun making a difficult square to Saturn had the sort of father who thought a weekly beating would 'make a man of him'. Because of this unpleasant early experience of male authority, he, metaphorically speaking, 'meets' his disciplinarian father when dealing with authority figures in general. He finds it difficult to trust them and resents the control they are capable of exerting over him. With the benefit of astrology's insights he is now aware of his own desire for control, inherited from his father – the aspect appears in his chart, remember. He now tries not to overreact. With difficult aspects like Moon/Saturn and Sun/Saturn, it is essential to recognise that some of the problem lies with our parent and the rest lies with ourselves. It is no easy task to resolve such inner conflicts to do with rejection and control, but by becoming aware of them, we at least allow into our lives the possibility of change.

An understanding of the birth chart can bring an awareness of the parental image we carry within us. It provides a unique starting point for a change in attitude. We can begin, if we have the Moon making a difficult aspect to Saturn, by allowing ourselves to appear vulnerable so that others see what is going on behind the cool facade. So, having looked at our charts and gained an awareness into a particular parental problem, we are then in a much better position to concentrate on expressing it positively rather than negatively. For example, a woman with a difficult aspect from Uranus to the Moon might feel that her own mother behaved in a detached manner and was never really comfortable in the maternal role. This particular aspect can indicate an uneasy relationship with traditional female roles, preferring the independence of remaining single and/or a career over marriage, the home and motherhood. Such a woman can now consciously decide to go ahead and have children, whilst making full use of creches and childminders, or forego motherhood altogether. For the majority of couples marrying up to say twenty years ago, children followed marriage as surely as day follows night. Obviously not every single woman born with her Moon making a difficult aspect to Uranus will be lacking in maternal instincts, but for those who do not 'feel the urge' to have children, an understanding of this aspect in the chart can indeed help us to make conscious choices which reflect our own inner truths and needs. Then we can begin to accept ourselves.

THE PARENTAL MARRIAGE

Our parents' marriage is a powerful image which we carry around inside us. In later life we tend to recreate this parental scenario since it is our first experience of relationship. One of the ways in which we do this is to be attracted to people who remind us of our parents. Robin Skynner, one of the pioneers of family therapy in this country, describes this uncanny mechanism in the book he co-wrote with John Cleese, *Families and How to Survive Them.* He recounts how in the 'Family Systems Exercise', trainee therapists who have never met each other previously choose partners and pair up with others whose family background, history and attitudes bear a remarkable similarity to their own. The mechanism which enables us to choose a partner with parental and family similarities operates unconsciously, although no-one is really sure how. The 'chemistry' explanation certainly doesn't do it justice, nor is it simply a case of interpreting our partner's body language.

Astrologer and Jungian analyst Liz Greene explains that, to us as children, our parents are our world and the source of life – they create us – and our continuing well-being depends on the harmony of their relationship. It is not so surprising, then, that we try to recreate this fruitful and most familiar relationship with someone else. If our parents' marriage was not harmonious, however, we may avoid 'serious' long-term relationships, or eschew relationships altogether. Such avoidance tactics inevitably involve cutting off from our natural feelings. Life can become lonely and unsatisfying. We are also effectively denying ourselves the opportunity of transforming an admittedly painful situation into a more constructive one. We cannot learn through experience if we won't allow ourselves the experience in the first place. Yet, life has a sneaky habit of causing the situation we have most feared and dreaded to fall right into our laps. The relationship you have put all your energy into avoiding may be right under your very nose! Sometimes our image of the parental marriage is like a reflection in a fairground hall of mirrors – we are capable of distorting it. Experiencing relationships for ourselves is an effective way of toning down the distortions and gaining a more balanced perspective.

THE PARENTAL MARRIAGE IN THE CHART

One of the main astrological indicators of how we experienced our parents' relationship is the relative strengths and weaknesses of the Sun and the Moon in the chart. The Sun represents the 'masculine' principle and usually signifies our experience of the father. The Moon representing the 'feminine' pole and usually indicates our experience of the Mother. The balance of power between the Sun and the Moon in the chart does seem to accord with our real-life experience of the balance of power in our parents' marriage. Most of us experience one of our parents as a stronger presence than the other. In difficult parental relationships, one is usually the 'goody' while the other is the 'baddy'. Since we are talking about our own charts here, we are describing part of ourselves as 'good' while the other part is 'bad'. Splitting off from the difficult aspects of our personalities does not allow us to become more integrated 'whole' individuals. Using astrology we can throw some light on how this internal marriage is operating in our lives, and how it is reflected in our own relationships.

I recently drew up the chart of a man who described his father as strict and unfeeling, while his mother was sensitive and highly emotional. He was much closer and more sympathetic to his mother who he felt had been misunderstood and made unhappy by his father. In the chart the Sun conjuncted Mars in an air sign, indicating a strong masculine element and a need for space. The Moon made two difficult aspects to Jupiter and Pluto, indicating intense but erratic emotions. In his own relationships he was drawn to emotional, highly strung women but found he had problems committing himself. So, women acted out his emotions for him while he appeared to be in control of them, like his father. Working with the insights afforded by the chart this man is now in a position to admit that he has intense feelings of his own, and that if he expresses them, he won't necessarily alienate his partner. There are women out there who actually enjoy being at the receiving end of a little passion and intensity!

Parental themes tend to draw people together and give them a chance to work with a difficult parental problem more creatively. For example, one couple I know both have the Sun making a difficult aspect to Neptune in their charts. Neptune, you will remember, is a vague, slippery planet. It tends to make things difficult to grasp, or they become idealised and unreal. In the case of this couple, they each felt their fathers were 'missing' from their lives in some way. The father of one was hardly ever around and eventually left the marriage to live in another country. The father of the other lived at home, but his presence was so nebulous that on an emotional level he was definitely absent.

It seems to hold true that we are all prone to turn our partners into our parents, however unpromising the material. Men tend to endow women with the attributes of their mothers, and women to experience men in terms of their fathers. In the case of my friends' relationship, the husband spends a lot of time travelling abroad. Both know about their charts and so are well aware of the danger of re-enacting their parents' marriage, with an absent husband replacing an absent father. They acknowledge that they both have a need to 'disappear' now and again and that this need not threaten the stability of their marriage. This may sound easy, but the relationship works because both partners have been brave enough to confront a potentially problematic situation and work with it creatively. When we stop experiencing our partner as one of our parents, their absence is no longer life-threatening.

The planetary relationship between the Sun and Moon in the chart can be a key to the state of our parents' relationship at birth. Although I have not found this to be true in every case, in some it can be particularly striking. I remember, for example, doing the chart of a friend's baby boy. A rather tense opposition between the Sun and the Moon in his chart reflected the estrangement of his parents at that time. Our parents' relationship, like any other relationship, does not, however, remain static. One baby girl's chart showed a harmonious aspect between the Sun and the Moon. Indeed, at the time of her birth her parents were very close, but they separated some eighteen months later and her mother left the country. The Moon in the child's chart, however, also opposes Saturn, indicating an undemonstrative mother and difficulties in childhood. The Sun, by contrast, conjuncts Venus showing a loving father, and she is in fact now living with her father full-time.

It is necessary, therefore, when looking at the image of the parental marriage in the chart to take all the astrological indicators I have mentioned into account – signs and rulers of the fourth and tenth houses, aspects made *by* the Sun and the Moon, and aspects *between* the Sun and the Moon. Often the chart throws up conflicting messages, as in the case of the baby girl, so it is important when reading the chart to be aware of ambiguities and contradictions. Our personalities and the relationships we experience are like Oscar Wilde's definition of the truth, 'rarely pure and never simple'.

OURSELVES AS PARENTS

Looking at our children's charts to gain some degree of insight into how our children experience us as parents is, as you can imagine, a tricky business. Seeing ourselves in the chart as a powerful and even manipulative Moon square Pluto mother, or a disappearing Sun opposite Neptune father is not, initially, going to make any of us feel particularly confident. However, no chart is entirely free from conflict, just as no individual life is going to be. Children are individuals and have opportunities to reinterpret the difficulties shown in the chart. As parents we often share the same signs and aspect patterns as our children. But we need to be aware of the way we dealt with the issues we inherited, on a psychological level, from our own parents. They have a profound influence on a growing child.

No single chart, however, is wholly problematic. There will also be harmonious aspects. In addition, looking at the astrological 'dialogue' or inter-aspects between the child's chart and the parents' can indicate areas of co-operation and mutual understanding. Recently, I was encouraged when I read a female astrologer's account of her relationship with her son. She said that the 'intense frustration' she felt 'at not being able to understand his little personal signals' had been considerably reduced when he was able to talk, because he could communicate (at age 2½ years) through words as well as simply through feelings. Although in his chart the Moon makes a difficult aspect to Neptune, which indicated to her that she might not read his needs very clearly, the constructive inter-chart aspects between her Moon and his Mercury make for good communication. The little boy also has the Moon in Gemini trine Mercury so he is, anyway, a regular chatterbox!

It must be stressed that aspects which, on one level, indicate the child's experience of the parents are part of the child's chart, meaning that they represent internal issues which the child will face as he or she grows older. Remember the man whose childhood experience of a strict disciplinarian father coloured his perception of authority figures in general as he grew older – he simply met his father in another form. We cannot protect our children from life nor, one could argue, from experiences necessary for their personal development as individuals. One mother, also an astrologer, knew her daughter was having an affair with a married man. Since the daughter's chart indicated that her mother was perceived as particularly Saturnian – strict and rather controlling – the mother had the wisdom not to come down too heavy on her daughter and exacerbate the problem. The daughter had to find out for herself the problems of being attracted to married men.

PUTTING YOUR FOOT IN IT – ASTROLOGY AND PSYCHOLOGY

This chapter has been written very much from a psychological perspective. When interpreting a chart it is very unwise to plunge headlong into parental and family issues without first acknowledging our own particular problems in these areas, and secondly, working with them. Exploring a person's experience of their parents and family can provoke emotional reactions. This can be confusing and distressing to both astrologer and client. In chapter 8 I will look at the responsibilities of the astrologer in more depth. At this point it must be stressed that when you first start to look at and interpret charts, it is highly inappropriate to jump straight into the psychological dynamics. Without some knowledge and experience of psychology, and insight into your own personal issues, wading into other people's will be like stepping into a lake full of dark and sticky treacle. Astrology works on many levels and defining the Sun, Moon, fourth and tenth houses in terms of our parental image is only one interpretation. Look back at the meanings of the planets in Chapter 4, and the Houses in Chapter 3, for other possibilities.

7.
ASTROLOGY AND RELATIONSHIPS

Give your hearts, but not into each other's keeping.
For only the hand of life can contain your hearts.
And stand together yet not too near together:
For the pillars of the temple stand apart,
And the oak tree and the cypress grow not
in each other's shadow.

Kahlil Gibran, *The Prophet*

Many of us are becoming aware, often painfully, that we have reached a transition point in the sphere of human relationships. The role of women in society has changed dramatically and both sexes seem bewildered as to how to react. Neither sex appears to be entirely comfortable with the fundamental alterations to the traditional patterns and attitudes many of us learned from our parents.

However, we cannot turn back the clock. In the UK in 1988 only 5 per cent of couples had the kind of marriage familiar to earlier generations, where the man goes out to work and the woman manages the home and brings up two children. The distinction between the roles of the sexes is becoming increasingly blurred as more women compete in the job market, buy their own houses, and have the power to choose whether to become parents, alone or in a couple. Astrology describes this period of transition as the 'dawning' of the Aquarian Age. Future-orientated Aquarius is an androgynous sign, meaning it combines both masculine and feminine attributes in a kind of astrological gender-bending. It is concerned with freedom, equality, independence and the role of the individual in society. Some men, mindful of the turning tide, are feeling more confident about developing their more 'feminine' sides by, for example, participating more fully in home life and bringing up children; or on an emotional level, by talking more openly about their feelings. Women do not have a monopoly on tenderness, warmth and kindness. The age of the 'Androgynous Manager' has arrived. Management, once tough-minded, is now required to express and accept emotions, while nurturing and supporting staff. The old stereotypes of the dominant male and the passive female belong to a declining race. But relationships are still at a confusing intermediate stage in this process of transformation.

We have not yet achieved the ideals of the new male-female relationship in which the qualities and attributes of both sexes are of equal value. The quest continues, but change does not come about without pressures or loss. American poet Robert Bly believes that the 'New Man', softer and more ecologically aware than his more macho, bread-winning, football-following predecessor, doesn't seem to have much life or energy. Women with demanding careers, on the other hand, are fast catching up with their highly stressed male counterparts in the heart-attack stakes. The 'New Age' of Aquarius is around for roughly another 2,000 years, but it has not yet got under way. We are at that strange, but exciting, place in-between.

A knowledge of astrology can help us understand our own capacity to form relationships so that we can better respond to this changing climate. Getting to know oneself, warts and all, is the first step in forming more fulfilling and more conscious attachments to others. If independence and individualism are key-words for the Aquarian Age, there may come a time when we no longer even live with our partners. So, perhaps we need to learn to live with ourselves. The birth chart provides a valuable tool in the process of self-acceptance and understanding.

When considering the issue of relationships, astrologers begin by establishing from the birth chart an individual's capacity for relationships and his or her attitude towards them. It is important to then consider the parental marriage and family background. Our parents provide the framework within which we first experience relationships. How we experience them and their marriage provides a lasting model for future relationships. The family and its influence in shaping the way we relate to other people and the outside world has already been fully discussed in the preceding chapter. A good place to start in this chapter on relationships is with the element balance of the birth chart.

RELATIONSHIPS AND THE ELEMENTS – FIRE, EARTH, AIR, WATER

The balance in a chart between the elements of fire, earth, air and water offers insight into the kind of temperament we have. I covered the elements briefly in Chapters 3 and 5 and explained that since there are ten planets, plus Ascendant, and only four types of signs (fire, earth, air, water), one or two elements are bound to predominate. It is particularly important to note the elements of the signs in which the relatively faster-moving 'personal' planets (Sun, Moon, Mercury, Venus, Mars, then Jupiter and Saturn) fall. Uranus, Neptune, and Pluto move very slowly through the zodiac so entire generations share the same placement. They are known as the 'outer' or 'transpersonal' planets. Pluto remained in the earth sign of Virgo from roughly June 1958 until August 1972. Broadly speaking, only if at least two of the personal planets, especially the Sun or Moon, and not forgetting the Ascendant, also fell in earth signs could you consider yourself an 'earthy' sort of person. So, the elements of the signs which contain these three 'transpersonal' planets should serve only to add weight to the element balance as already shown in the chart by the 'personal' planets and the Ascendant.

By offering a guide to our basic nature, identifying the strongest element in the chart acts as a guide to how we might express ourselves most naturally in a relationship. It shows where we feel 'in our element'. For example, a woman with a planetary emphasis in the air signs (Gemini, Libra and Aquarius) will, generally speaking, find greater fulfillment in a relationship where she can mix freely on a social level, and pursue interests outside the relationship. A man, say, with a watery emphasis, such as the Sun in Cancer, Venus and Mars in Scorpio, will want to be involved in whatever his partner is doing in order to feel emotionally secure in the relationship. You can imagine that this man is going to have problems with our airy, independent woman who might feel stifled by what she would experience as his clinginess. On the other hand, a man with an emphasis on the fire signs, such as Sun and Jupiter in Sagittarius with Aries rising, might suddenly get enthused over a new scheme or sidetracked by a chance meeting. Both of these result in him missing the start of the performance his partner with Sun in Taurus and Moon conjunct the Ascendant in Virgo had carefully chosen. Fiery types prefer to do things spontaneously and fail to understand why earthy types like to have everything under control and worked out in advance.

Conflicting Elements

Just to make matters more complicated, our birth charts often contain two conflicting temperaments within them. Using the concept of the chart as a cast of characters we can find out and recognise those parts of ourselves which conflict and cause problems in our relationships with others. For example, a person whose chart has the Sun and Ascendant in Cancer but the Moon in Aquarius is likely to want a close relationship which provides an emotional anchor, but at the same time need periods of unrestrained freedom and new experiences. Another example of such 'double messages' in a chart was a female client who had the Sun in Taurus opposite Moon in Scorpio and making a difficult aspect to the planet Mars. Her earthy Taurus side enjoyed the simple pleasures of nice dinners, relaxing evenings after work, finding comfort in a stable home life. Her Scorpio Moon, however, wanted to probe beneath the surface and generally stir up the ordered world she had created by means of emotional outbursts which she found very difficult to control. Astrology helps to make us aware of such inherent contradictions, and with awareness comes change. There are times when it is appropriate for my female client to take the lid off her feelings, but equally there are times when this might be destructive. We can try, beginning with the birth chart, to unlearn patterns of reacting which have proved unhelpful. This takes time and energy, but isn't your relationship worth it?

WORKING WITH IMBALANCES

A knowledge of the elements of the chart is beneficial in many ways. Firstly it can lead to an acceptance of conflicting temperaments within us. Secondly it encourages us to understand others who are temperamentally different to us and, hopefully, allow them to be themselves. Thirdly, through relationships with people who are strong in an element which is weak in our charts, we can gain a degree of insight into those parts of ourselves we are only dimly aware of. For example, a woman with a very watery chart learnt to take things less personally through a relationship with an airy, more objective man. This made social situations much less of a strain. For his part, he came to realise that people could not always explain their reactions rationally in words of two syllables. He became more tolerant of the feelings of others both at home and at work. However, if the watery lady had allowed the airy man do all the talking and take all the decisions, she would never have developed her own capacity for objectivity and detachment. Similarly if the airy man had always allowed his watery partner to play the emotional characters in their particular script, he would have lost the opportunity to re-establish contact with his own feelings.

A relationship between an earthy and a fiery type could easily fall into the same trap. The earthy partner may fear and resist change on the basis of better the devil you know than the devil you don't know. Then, those opportunities which the fiery partner would have eagerly grasped will be gone, leaving the earthy type stuck in a rut. Earth can learn from fire to be more spontaneous and less fearful about looking would-be gift horses in the mouth. Fire can learn from earth that snap decisions and wading in boots and all may lead to trouble. The intuition of the fiery type is not always 100 per cent accurate. Like the Sagittarian arrows, when they go astray they can be very wide of the mark indeed. Earth appreciates the virtues of deliberating and taking past experience into account.

GETTING IN TOUCH

Because they feel uncomfortable, the element or elements lacking in the birth chart can erupt at the most inopportune times. The person who lacks water, the feeling element, may be unaware of the depth of their feelings until a relationship ends and he or she finds they have completely lost their cool, pouring out their hearts to anyone who will listen. A relationship with a more watery

type who was more comfortable expressing feelings just
might have helped by making the airy type aware of his or
her hidden side. I have lost count of the number of times I
have heard people say something along the lines of 'My
boyfriend or husband or lover is a Pisces and I'm a Libra.
We're not meant to get on.' Apart from the obvious fact
that there is much more to a person than his or her Sun
sign, it perpetuates the myth that only signs of the same
element are compatible. A quick glance at the lonely
hearts column in a magazine produced half a dozen
examples of fire, water, and air Sun signs (perhaps the
earth signs felt it was too risky) all seeking partners of the
same element. They don't know what they're missing!
Hopefuly it has become clear that we have much to learn
from partners who are distinctly unlike us. So please do
not condemn your relationship at the first signs of stress,
or even before it has begun. Get to know your own chart,
and that of your partner. Look at your relative strengths
and weaknesses in different elements to see where you can
learn from each other.

THE INNER PARTNER OR FINDING HOOKS TO HANG UP OUR PICTURES

You cannot tell from the birth chart whether a person is
male or female as both sexes have the same signs and
planets. Aries and Mars are more masculine or yang, while
others, like Cancer and the Moon, are more feminine or yin.
There are many men with a more 'feminine' bias to the
chart, and women with a more 'masculine' energy.
Feminine, in this sense, does not mean pertaining to
women exclusively, nor is masculine reserved solely for the
male sex. Need I say here that astrology does appreciate
the differences between men and women! When
interpreting a chart it is essential to know whether it
belongs to a man or a woman. We are all aware of the
biological differences and their profound effects, yet it is
difficult to define the precise meaning of 'masculine' and
'feminine'. Poet and writer Peter Redgrove offers one

interesting summary, 'The feminine spirit inclines towards completeness but not perfection, and the masculine spirit inclines towards perfection but not completeness.'

However to return to the question of relationships, our choice of partner is coloured by the element balance of the chart as explained above. Equally, if not more important, are the sign and aspects to the Sun, the Moon, Venus and Mars. To a lesser extent, the sign on, and any planets in, the seventh house of the chart can offer a guide to what we are looking for in a partner. At the risk of over-simplification, a woman with Cancer rising and Capricorn, the opposite sign, on the cusp of the seventh house, might be drawn to older men, or more traditional 'tailored' types, or father figures. This, however, is not a strong enough indication in itself. The relationship 'signature' would have to be reinforced elsewhere in the woman's chart, by, for instance, her Venus aspecting Saturn, ruling planet of Capricorn. Sounds complicated, but then relationships are. Why two people are together cannot be explained by some vague indefinable term like 'chemistry'. There are many factors at work.

GIVING IT ALL AWAY

In traditional astrology women are said to look for men who embody the essence of their more 'masculine' Sun or Mars signs. This means a woman with Sun in Aries and Mars in Leo would go for a dynamic, entrepreneurial type complete with fast car and trendy clothes. Men, on the other hand, are said to look for women who will express the more 'feminine' side of the chart. So a man with the Moon in Libra and Venus in Gemini would be attracted to vivacious, sociable women with culture and taste. Increasingly I am becoming aware that there is less and less evidence to support this neat theory of sexual stereotypes. Men are quite capable of identifying with their Moon sign, and looking elsewhere for someone to express their Sun and Mars signs. Many men are turned on by dynamic, exuberant females who compete for recognition in the outside world. Women can and do express the qualities of their Sun sign and may seek out a more 'feminine' (not the same as effeminate) male who feels very comfortable cooking, painting, working in a caring profession, or nurturing seedlings in the garden.

In reality the planets or signs we admire or which attract us are often strong in our own charts. A male client told me he found Scorpio women very attractive and went on to describe their particular qualities. In fact he himself had a Scorpio Ascendant, strengthened by two other planets close to it and in the same sign. However, he didn't appear to recognise in himself any of the magnetic yet mysterious qualities which so attracted him in Scorpio women. This phenomenon is called projection and manifests in all relationships especially at the beginning, and often for the duration. What happens is that, like my client, we have an inner picture of what we find alluring and then find someone who provides a suitable hook for us to hang up our picture. This inner image, however, is a part of ourselves that we have failed to recognise. So we get our partners to embody it for us. Disappointment inevitably follows when we find that our partner doesn't come up to our expectations. In many cases we wonder what we ever saw in them in the first place. The person we are looking for does not actually exist – except of course in our own imagination.

An analysis of the birth chart can throw some light on which parts of ourselves we don't own up to and which we hook on to others. In the section on the elements (pp. 123–125) I mentioned that we are often drawn to partners who possess the element which is weak in our own charts. Projection occurs when we expect them to live out all the attributes of this element. The person with very little water can get hooked up with a partner who is very emotional. This way the partner has the feelings for both parties in the relationship. You can probably think of your own examples like the couple where one is never angry and the other seems to shout a lot, or the person who is always cheerful married to a partner who is depressive. Such relationships do survive, but the collusion that exists means that particular dimensions of each partner's personality never get a chance to develop. For example I had a male client who complained that his wife was depressive, abusive and violent. In his chart I found the Moon sitting right next to Pluto, making a hard aspect to Mercury, planet of communication. This indicated that my client had hidden, turbulent feelings himself which, if provoked, could have come out as insensitive emotional outbursts. Without an outlet such negative feelings could easily lead to internal anger and depression. It was as if my client's wife had provided the hook for the difficult aspects of her husband's emotions and lived out his unacknowledged anger and depression for him. He was surprised to discover the existence of that potentially destructive sub-personality in his own chart. I am not suggesting that astrology by itself can solve this man's marital problems, but it can point the way towards taking responsibility for his less attractive characteristics rather than laying all the blame at his wife's door.

THE ASTROLOGICAL CLOCK – BEGINNINGS, ROUGH PATCHES, ENDINGS, TRANSFORMATIONS

Testing Times

When certain planets – Saturn, Uranus, Neptune, Pluto – make contact at a particular point in their cycle with our 'relating' planets, especially the Moon and Venus, we are more likely to begin, end or experience difficulties in our relationships. Saturn aspecting the Moon or Venus can test a relationship. If the relationship has a strong foundation, it will survive. Saturn has a propensity for putting obstacles in our path while focusing on our emotional sore spots. I lost count of the number of times a friend's relationship collapsed in ruins only to rise up again, when Saturn contacted her Venus. Just to make matters worse, Saturn made a difficult aspect to her boyfriend's Venus a year later and the whole disheartening scenario was re-enacted. Yet they are still together. On the other hand, when Saturn moved over a client's Descendant he reluctantly acknowledged the depressing reality of his relationship and, mustering up all his courage, he brought it to an end. If the relationship lacks a solid basis of love and trust, it may, like this one, go under. Yet, paradoxically, the shared experience of a testing Saturn transit can deepen the bond between two people. Since Saturn symbolises the need for structures or contracts, it can herald the beginning of a particular kind of relationship. I established a business partnership when Saturn contacted Venus in my chart.

Waking Up and Shaking Up
Uranus can literally awaken us to the existence of another person and make an exciting start to a relationship. I have seen people rush into marriage under this aspect. On the other hand, Uranus can shake up a relationship to such an extent that it fractures, like the man whose Moon, his emotional anchor, underwent a difficult aspect from this planet. At the same time, his girlfriend left their shared home. On another level, the Moon can refer to the physical body. A female client felt out of touch with her body when Uranus made a stressful aspect to her Moon. During this difficult time a sensitive and supportive partner would have been a tremendous help. Another female client with Uranus aspecting her Venus was able to put her relationship on a different footing. She realised that once she stopped regarding the relationship as a lifelong commitment, the pressure on both partners would be eased. She said this realisation came like 'a bolt from the blue', after which the relationship definitely improved. A knowledge of astrology is helpful at such stages in a relationship because it can provide insight into the planetary energies at work. Working with them rather than against them, while they last, helps us to look at our relationships more creatively.

Enchantment and Letting Go

Neptune aspecting the Moon or Venus can enchant us so
that we fall under another's spell. Many love affairs begin
under the magical influence of this planet. People declare
that they were 'meant' to be together or they have 'known
each other before'. Once this spell has worn off the real
world of whose turn it is to do the washing up intrudes and
then more effort is needed on both sides to make the
relationship work. Sometimes we discover to our
amazement that we have fallen in love with an ass, like
Titania in *A Midsummer Night's Dream*. Neptune often
asks that we let go or make sacrifices in relationships. One
female friend was made painfully aware of the need to give
up her still-married lover when Neptune was going over
the Descendant of her chart. There is a saying that if
something is yours, it will come back to you. Her story had
a happy ending – her partner left his wife and came to her,
but not before she had consciously let him go.

Obsessions and Endings

Pluto aspecting the relating planets or the Descendant
can often bring obsessive, compulsive or secret
relationships. We can become obsessed by another person
or embark on an illicit affair. I know two women who
launched into secret affairs and admitted feeling 'driven'
and out of control when Pluto aspected their Venus and
Descendant respectively. Another male client ended his
relationship when Pluto moved over his Venus but, in
keeping with a planet named after the god of hidden
treasure, he met someone else and found a very well-paid
job! Pluto, god of death, can signify the end of a
relationship. Astrology can help at such times by making
us aware of the need to leave behind a relationship when it
has been outgrown. Accepting endings makes room for
new beginnings. At the same time astrologers understand
the painful side of Pluto and the need for a period of
mourning. Fortunately, Pluto transits do not go on for
ever. All the planets I have mentioned in this section have
cycles which have a discernible beginning and end.

Astrology can help by giving us an indication of the timescale involved.

WORK AND PROFESSIONAL RELATIONSHIPS

It is very unlikely that you will have access to the information necessary to draw up the whole chart of your colleagues at work or professional contacts. Asking for such information could be seen as an intrusion, unless of course you run your own business! Most people, however, know their Sun sign and will happily tell you their birthday. If you are familiar with the basics of astrology you can extract quite a lot of information from this one detail. If not, knowing a colleague's Sun sign can still be illuminating. Most of us get on with others who share our Sun signs since we have something in common. Yet if we familiarise ourselves with the other eleven signs, it can lead to a greater tolerance of others. We each contain all twelve signs in our charts. Getting to know people who embody the attributes of a sign to which we cannot relate or actively dislike is a useful experience. If someone at work continually irritates us or rubs us up the wrong way, it is often a sure sign that they have great deal in common with one of the roles in our own cast of characters that we'd rather not discuss. We don't all paint pretty pictures, some of those we keep in the basement are fairly gruesome. It is much easier to hang these on other people's walls than have them on our own as a constant reminder.

I mentioned in Chapter 5 that we usually have difficulty with people who were born under the sign opposite our own Sun sign. Opposites can attract or repel, but like the yin-yang symbol, they each contain a part of the other. So when we declare, like one female Sagittarian client, that we 'can't stand Geminis', it is a part of ourselves that we refuse to accept. Another female client said that she 'just couldn't work with Pisceans'. An analysis of her chart showed that she had no planets in the element of water. Pisces is perhaps the most fluid and emotional of the water signs. What this woman was really saying was that there was something that bothered her about people who were emotionally changeable and worked according to their own inner rhythms. Obviously Pisceans are subject to the same deadlines as everyone else. However, my Aries client with strong Capricorn found the suggestion that she might not barge in head first and relax her control a little made some sense. Treating future Piscean colleagues with sensitivity would get her a much better response as well as hopefully putting her in touch with her undeveloped 'feeling' side.

Another Capricorn friend had problems with his driving instructor. Knowing Saturn-ruled Capricorn's need to be in control of the situation I wasn't surprised to find that what really bothered him was the dual-control mechanism of the instructor's car! Capricorns do seem to want to do everything their own way. Unfortunately, driving instructors also have a job to do. Another man with a close Sun and Saturn conjunction couldn't understand why he was losing staff at a rate of knots. He tended to over-react dramatically whenever one of his employees acted on their own initiative and introduced a new idea, or questioned one of his decisions. He needed to be in complete control since he trusted no-one else's judgement. However, this took up an enormous amount of time and energy. He had not yet learned that maintaining a low profile and giving his staff more responsibility might not only bring out the best in them, but also lighten his own load. You may need to prove to colleagues or bosses with strong Saturn or Capricorn that the place isn't going to fall apart while their back is turned.

A knowledge of your colleagues' Sun signs can indeed be helpful in the delicate sphere of office politics. Capricorn's opposite number, Cancer, enjoys playing a 'motherly' role in the workplace. In one of the places I work, two people, a man and a woman, liked to buy biscuits for everybody. With the Sun in Cancer, they both understood the importance of feeding people and making the workplace more homely. We aren't obliged to eat all of Cancer's offerings, but we can acknowledge that food, for them, is a form of emotional, as well as physical nourishment. Aquarians may prefer to buy their own biscuits! Aquarian colleagues may appear friendly, but don't expect them to eat lunch with you every day or be enthusiastic about office outings and parties. Don't take it personally – Aquarians need space and may be quite content working away at their desk in the corner while the rest of the office is crammed into the nearest pub. When your Sagittarian boss exclaims that she loves your work and is delighted with your new scheme, do not think that your promotion is a *fait accompli*. A knowledge of this sign's basic characteristics tells you immediately that Sagittarians are quickly enthused, as well as being prone to exaggeration. You would be well advised to strike while the iron is hot and make alternative plans for the future. Otherwise you will only feel let down when someone else becomes flavour of the month. And if you know anything about Virgos, you'll have realised the importance of checking everything down to the last detail. And frequent long lunch hours won't be at all popular as Virgos are conscientious types and to them, an hour means 60 minutes not 75. Use astrology to get to know your workmates better and realise and appreciate that everyone brings something different to their working environment.

SYNASTRY OR CHART COMPARISON

Synastry is the comparison of one astrological chart with another. It is a technique most often requested by couples who wish to explore their compatibility. This can happen, for example, at the beginning of a relationship out of curiosity, or later if problems arise. However it can be a valuable tool in families where there are conflicts between different members. It can also offer insight into a prospective partnership or joint venture with another person or persons. Synastry works. In one study reported in the *Astrological Journal*, 1,000 married couples filled in a questionnaire to determine how happy they were. Ten very high-scoring couples and ten very low-scorers were chosen for analysis. Ten astrologers were given the birth charts of these 20 and asked to determine which were the happy and which the unhappy couples. The same task was set ten psychologists who were given the results of standard personality tests done on the same 20 couples. The astrologers scored considerably higher than chance, and their findings were fairly accurate.

When asked to compare two charts, astrologers first assess both people's capacity for relationship as reflected in their birth charts. A lack of the 'feeling' element water, for example, or difficult aspects from the planet Uranus to the 'relationship-orientated' planets like the Moon and Venus, could point to a tendency to cut off from the feelings. Then the element balance of the charts will be assessed. As I have already mentioned, signs of the same element get on, but two people with an emphasis on the same element may experience difficulties. For example two people of an earthy temperament may get stuck since each is waiting for the other to make a move. Two people with a concentration on air may communicate very well on an intellectual level, but the emotional and physical dimensions of the relationship may not prove so fulfilling. One partner may look elsewhere either for someone who is more in tune with their feelings, or someone who is more sensual. Astrologers can not magically inject another element into this airy relationship. However we can identify and throw some light on the problem area. We might suggest to the airy couple that they climb out of their heads occasionally and follow less intellectual pursuits. There are other equally enjoyable ways of relating which use less verbal forms of communication like massage, dancing, cooking or listening to music together.

Interplanetary Contact

The dialogue between one person's planets and another's is the most important factor in comparing charts. Someone's Jupiter, an expansive planet, making a harmonious aspect or conjuncting your Moon signifies

quite simply that your partner will make you feel good.
Since your Moon hits your partner's Jupiter, expressing
feelings shouldn't pose too much of a problem. All
contacts, however, have a positive and a negative
dimension. In the charts of one couple I saw, the man's
Saturn was sitting on the woman's Sun. Sun or
Moon/Saturn contacts are said to crop up frequently in
long-term relationships. Saturn has a bonding nature. In
the first year or two of my client's relationship the woman
had experienced the man as grounded, stable, protective –
all very positive qualities of Saturn. Later on she said he
was too self-controlled, conventional and lacked
imagination – the less attractive Saturnian traits. When
the man eventually felt rejected and proposed to end the
relationship, however, the woman felt very insecure. She
flipped back into wanting to experience him as stable and
protective! The relationship ended, but on a more realistic
note with greater understanding on both sides of the
dynamics between them and the element of projection
involved.

When two planets aspect each other across charts their
energies fuse. It is not a simple division of planets like a
division of labour – you have all the Saturn and I'll have
all the Sun. In the above relationship responsibility for
both energies must be acknowledged. My female client
also has Saturn operating in her own chart, both positively
and negatively. She too can be capable and realistic, and
she did eventually find these qualities in herself. What
most attracts us in another can end up being what we
most hate about them! If you find yourself consistently
drawn to partners who seem adventurous and independent
only to find that they forget to include you in their plans,
give astrology a try. You might just uncover your own
hidden need for freedom and new horizons, and begin to
find out why you are afraid to express it. Why not begin a
voyage of self-discovery round your birth chart and lessen
the chances of repeating painful patterns.

The Composite Chart

If you want to explore your relationship further, a composite chart can be drawn up. However it is beyond the scope of this book to explain the precise calculations involved. Put simply, the composite chart is a single chart which combines both partners' charts. It meshes together the energies and essences of the charts of two individuals to show a shared energy pattern. Astrologers who have many years of experience with the composite chart have found it to be a productive and reliable technique when working with relationships.

ASTROLOGY AND SELF-AWARENESS

We live on a small planet where there is more conflict worldwide than we can cope with. Astrology offers a unique tool for self-awareness which can lead to greater tolerance in all our relationships, in or out of the home. Conflict can be a dynamic force in our own personalities and in our human relationships. However, intolerance and coercion are not the best ways to manage it. Co-operation and consensus are much more creative. A knowledge of astrology allows us access and insight into our own inner conflicts. If we can then face the truth about ourselves and take responsibility for it, we are less likely to lay the blame for our own shortcomings at another's feet. If we can be more tolerant of our inner contradictions, we stand a good chance of allowing others to be themselves. And we can learn to appreciate differences rather than condemning others for them. In many situations where there is conflict, the people concerned have little mutual understanding. 'But you don't understand me' is an oft-heard complaint. A knowledge of the energies at work in the birth chart gives us an opportunity for understanding. As I have already said we all share the same twelve signs and ten planets. Making a conscious effort towards acceptable future personal relationships might just help towards solving conflict on an international level. Stranger things have happened! As Erich Fromm so wisely said, 'Love is an act of faith, and whoever is of little faith is also of little love.'

8.
LIFE CYCLES AND TIMES OF CHANGES

THE ASTROLOGICAL CLOCK

Everything must change, nothing stays the same. It is one of the few things in life of which we can be absolutely certain. We are born, we reach sexual maturity, we reproduce, and eventually we die. Throughout the unfolding of this natural cycle, we may be conscious of the ebbing and flowing of our own inner rhythms. Sometimes our boat sails smoothly with the tide, at other times it seems to be wildly off course, or even stuck on a sandbank. At some point we all experience a rough crossing and need

time to repair the damage before we can continue on our
life's journey.

As I hope I have shown astrology is a philosophy which
identifies correspondences between the cycles of the
planets in space and time and experience and events in an
individual's life here on earth. A psychological approach to
astrology seeks not to predict events but rather to
encourage, first of all, awareness of the consequences of
our actions and attitudes, and secondly, to discover what
they mean on an inner level. However, casting a watchful
eye over imminent planetary movements is a kind of
astrological weather forecasting – after all, if rain is on the
way, it is a good idea to carry an umbrella. We cannot
trade in our chart for another, but we can use it as a
navigational aid. We can learn to go with the flow rather
than against it, or, as the Zen Buddhists would say, 'Don't
push the river.' How many times have we said, 'Oh, if only
I'd waited' or 'If only I had taken that opportunity when it
was offered.' Timing is very important, as everyone, from
actors to acrobats, knows. Surely we would all benefit from
a better sense of timing.

Time and tide, so the saying goes, wait for no man.
Astrology can help to identify those times when it is
appropriate to make your move, and, equally importantly,
those times when it is better not to make a move at all.
Astrologers achieve this by studying the actual planetary
cycles in the heavens and plotting them on your birth
chart. When assessing how the different planetary
energies are operating in your life, what happened in the
past has a significant bearing on the present and the
future. Astrologers map out planetary movements on your
chart to see which sensitive points have been, are being, or
will be triggered off, as the planet moves through its orbit.
The 'sensitive points' in your chart are, broadly speaking,
the Sun, Moon, Ascendant and planets (especially the
personal planets) plus the Midheaven. It is also important
to note when a planet moves out of one house in your chart
and into the next. When orbiting planets make contact
with such points in your chart, they give an indication of

trends and issues likely to arise in your life. On one level, they enable the astrologer to see you in context – to see 'where you're at'. When a planet makes contact, it sets up a circuit of energy which modifies our inner rhythms. Sometimes this energy is accompanied by emotional and psychological changes, changes on an inner level. At other times things seem to 'happen' to us in the outside world, things we did not see coming. For the astrologer they are one and the same thing, the inner reflects the outer and vice versa.

The movement of a planet over sensitive points in your chart is called a transit. So, when the planet Pluto contacts the Sun in your birth chart, Pluto is said to be transiting your Sun. This transit offers the opportunity for major spring cleaning in your life, a chance to divest yourself of old, outworn attitudes and beliefs. If a planet, say Uranus, crosses your Descendant into the seventh house of the chart, it is said to be transiting that house. This transit would tend to focus your awareness on issues of freedom versus dependency in relationships. You can find out where the actual planets are by consulting a set of astronomical tables known as an 'ephemeris'. If there is one thing astrologers and astronomers do agree on, it is the positions of the planets at any given time.

Implicit in the word 'transit' is the idea of something passing through. The planets do in fact pass through, or over, our charts. They never take up permanent residence. The outer planets – Uranus, Neptune and Pluto – move relatively slowly; for instance Uranus takes approximately 84 years to complete its cycle. This means that Uranus will return to the place it occupied at your birth when you reach the grand old age of 84. Saturn takes between 28 and 30 years to complete a circuit of your chart. This completion point is of particular importance. For astrologers, not your 21st, but, on average, your 29th birthday, signifies your coming of age. The years from 28 to 30 mark a turning point in your life. It is then that you emerge as an individual from the cocoon of the family, but more about this later. What I would like to point out at this stage is the importance of such planetary transits in our lives. They present an opportunity, lasting only a finite length of time, for growth and development which we can integrate into our life as a whole. Particular aspects made by the slower, outer planets in your chart may only happen once in our lifetime. Life is no dress rehearsal, so why miss your particular cue? It could be the performance of your life.

THE SATURN CYCLE

The number seven is connected wth a process of structure and evolution in time. We have our seven days of the week, then the cycle begins again. Shakespeare talked of the seven ages of man whose life-span was measured as three score years and ten. Until the discovery of Uranus, there were only seven known planets (five plus the Sun and the Moon) in the horoscope. Saturn is the seventh planet and its roughly 28-year cycle can be divided into four significant sub-cycles, each lasting seven years. How we relate to the energy symbolised by Saturn gives an indication of how well, or badly, we structure, or experience structure, in our lives.

The period from birth to around age seven years is a crucial stage in a child's development. During this time Saturn moves round the circle of the chart to the point where it makes a square or 90 degree aspect to the place it occupied at your birth. As the old Jesuit saying goes, 'Give me a child until he's seven and he's mine for life.' Throughout this stage of life, a child learns about authority and boundaries, both of which are symbolised by Saturn. Saturn in the chart can often signify the father – through him we usually experience discipline. (If this was how you experienced your mother then for father read mother.) We tend to learn from the father just how far we can go, through him we discover where to draw the line. If we are not given clear boundaries by the age of seven, or if they are too emphatically drawn, we can overstep the mark later in life and run into problems with authority. If a strong bond is not established with the father because of, for instance, his absence, then our basic sense of trust suffers. This can manifest itself as, for example, low self-esteem, doing things to please the father, or being attracted in later life to someone who is not available. One female client who married very young realised much later that she had chosen her husband precisely because her father approved of him. She did it to please her father, not herself. Needless to say, the marriage was short-lived.

Saturn's next seven-year sub-cycle finishes when it arrives at the point where it is opposite, or 180 degrees from, the place it occupied at an individual's birth. From age seven onwards school and learning play a major role in our lives. We spend more time away from our parents and learn about authority, responsibility and status. Problems at this stage can result in feelings of inferiority or hiding our abilities if they don't appear to be approved by family or friends. We want to be different, but we also want to conform. We begin to question our parents' authority and experiment with our own by telling younger children what to do. If events, such as moving house, are not explained adequately to us at this stage, they can provoke feelings of insecurity. The present may always seem relatively uncertain.

From our fourteenth year onwards we embark on adolescence. During this period, which ends roughly at age 21 years, Saturn moves another 90 degrees, or three-quarters of the way around the birth chart. This can be an upsetting and confusing time, marked by tremendous changes on a physical, sexual and emotional level. We are unsure whether we belong in the world of children or adults. We learn about responsibility and the importance of being accepted by our peers. We look outside the family for role models, from pop stars to football players. We begin to rebel against our parents' attitudes and values in order to separate from them. Some of us can't wait to leave home to find work when our parents want us to study. Some of us want to pursue further education when our parents would prefer us to go out and find a job. Others make the separation via early marriages or setting up house, with or without our parents' blessing.

From age 21 to the conclusion of the first Saturn cycle (the Saturn return) at 28 to 30 years, we look for more permanent relationships. We are viewed by society as adults and regard supporting ourselves financially as a more serious, long-term proposition. We begin to get a sense of our own identity away from the family. Being accepted by friends becomes more important, although not at the expense of our own personal attitudes and beliefs. Now is the time to shed those attitudes which you no longer share with your parents but have hung on to in order to please them. Early marriages may break up around age 28 to 30; others get married for the first time; others have children as we begin to get a sense of accepting responsibility for our own lives. The experience of Saturn making a complete circuit of our charts is a maturing one.

The Saturn return is perhaps the most popular time to come for an astrological consultation. It marks the beginning of a new cycle and heralds a period of choice. At this stage we begin to have a much clearer and more realistic idea of who we are and the kind of direction we would like to take. Life is no longer full of endless possibilities. In keeping with the restraining and realistic nature of Saturn, we accept that our choices are indeed limited. It is a time to face reality and consolidate our experience. Now is the moment to clear away any dead wood and concentrate on those things which are working for us. We need courage to draw the line and take a long, hard look at ourselves. This may mean giving up our plans, whether they involve partners or careers, if they lack a solid base in reality. If we have not really severed the umbilical cord, then this is the time to do it. It is time to strengthen our own boundaries to develop a stronger sense of self.

How we deal with the next twenty-eight to thirty years will depend very much on our progress so far. If we persist in clinging on to our family, we will continue to espouse their values and attitudes. If we haven't thought through such issues ourselves, these inherited opinions may sound a shade unconvincing, even to us. If we remain dependent on our parents we may wind up marrying someone just like them and still not cut the ties. At this time in our lives we become vaguely aware that we aren't immortal and that time is of the essence. Many people hope to 'make it' by 30, not thinking about what to do if they don't.

By studying the sign, house position and aspects to Saturn in your birth chart, astrologers can help you through this difficult time. A knowledge of astrology enables us to focus on particular issues or areas of conflict. If problems are not identified at this stage, the same conflicts will persist but the pattern becomes more deeply ingrained, making attempts at resolution much more difficult. Saturn often signifies where we are most vulnerable or where we feel least confident. Paradoxically, it can be those very areas which are our strengths in disguise. Looking through astrology's lens during this period gives helpful insights into areas of potential growth and development. It takes courage to face up to one's limitations but this is the time to start living in the real world.

THE ASTROLOGICAL MID-LIFE CRISIS

Just as we astrologers have our own ideas about the coming-of-age period, so we also identify that tricky turning point, popularly known as the mid-life crisis. This is another favourite time to come for an astrological consultation and usually happens roughly between the age of 40 and 42, although it can happen as early as 38. This depends on the time taken for the planet Uranus to reach the point directly opposite the place it occupied at your birth. This period marks a major turning point in our life cycle. Put very bluntly, it begins to dawn on us that our days are numbered and that our youthful aspirations are unlikely now ever to come to fruition. This, as you can imagine, can throw us into a panic and herald a period of rather frantic searching for our lost youth. It may feel very much like a last fling. One manifestion of this urge on the part of the male population is to take off with much younger women. Perhaps the 'toy boy' phenomenon is an equivalent female reaction! It's now or never, we cry, and make dramatic changes in relationships, jobs or careers, as we realise we have been in the wrong one for years. Two women I know decided to give up careers in publishing and the arts respectively and train as psychotherapists. The time of the Uranus opposition affects people in different ways. People who have led relatively stable lives decide, like one man, to leave a well-paid job, sell up and travel round the country in a dormobile. Others who have never really settled decide to put down roots. Old familiar patterns seem stale and restrictive. Marriages tend to stabilise or break up as we wake up to wishes and desires we didn't realise were there all the time.

This is indeed a time of great change, but it is also a time of opportunity. An astrological consultation at this stage can offer guidance by clarifying confusion about relationships, jobs or vocation. The birth chart can indicate where our relative strengths and weaknesses lie, and in what areas we can develop them more fully. Panic tends to blind us to the fact that we have more time or more options than we think. Taking time to study the chart and consider our situation may prevent rash behaviour. If a marriage breaks down we can use the chart to explore what this means on an inner level. We might discover that parts of ourselves could not be expressed within the relationship. On the other hand, the symptoms may surface in the relationship but the problem lies elsewhere. The sudden freedom this brings can indeed be frightening but it can provoke a turning inward or a more spiritual awareness during this second half of life. Uranus teaches the wisdom of facing the truth about ourselves and living out those parts of our personalities we have kept in the closet.

TURNING POINTS AND THE ROLE OF THE ASTROLOGER

There are many reasons why people seek out astrologers. Some want confirmation that they are on the right track in terms of career, some are at a crossroads and confused as to which direction to take. Some are going through a painful emotional crisis – the break up of a close relationship, or the loss of a friend, parent or loved one. Some come out of pure curiosity, others ostensibly for a 'character reading'. Often the real reason for the visit soon becomes clear – they may feel depressed and alone, or there may be an underlying health crisis.

No-one likes to admit they have real problems, or feel they have failed in some way. A visit to the astrologer is a less threatening option than counselling or psychotherapy. Having a chart reading is something anyone can do for themselves in the short term. It is your choice to consult an astrologer and it is entirely up to you whether you take it any further. There is no obligation to go back to the astrologer for a return visit, unless of course you want to. You need never see him or her again for the rest of your life. If you don't like, or don't altogether accept, what the astrologer has to say, no-one need know. Alternatively you can make jokes about your reading later and dismiss the whole thing as preposterous nonsense. Strangely enough, I have not yet met anyone from this last group. Perhaps that in itself is a sign that astrology is being taken more seriously and attracting a different kind of client.

My own personal clients have ranged from professionals – barristers, doctors, film producers and company chairmen – to less affluent nurses, students, secretaries, and those who have chosen to drop out of society altogether. Everyone whose chart I have been privileged to read has left with, at most, a serious degree of respect for astrology or, at least, a feeling that there is something in it after all.

THE MODERN ASTROLOGER – A CHALLENGING ROLE

It has probably become clear while reading the latter part of this book, that astrologers can find themselves in some pretty tricky situations. It is not unusual to find that your client has a severe drink problem, is seriously depressed, or has been tested for the AIDS virus and found to be HIV positive. In such cases the astrologer takes on the role of counsellor. Yet even in less extreme circumstances, the problems which are brought to the astrologer require an understanding of human psychology and a willingness to deal with issues of an emotional or even spiritual nature. Talking about parental problems (as I pointed out in Chapter 7) can provoke deep emotional reactions. A basic understanding of psychological concepts is necessary here if both astrologer and client are not to feel out of their depth. A reading given by an astrologer who consciously works with its psychological dimension will, to my mind, be a more complete and satisfying experience.

Astrologers appear divided on the subject of counselling or therapeutic experience. I would ally myself with those who advocate personal experience of counselling or therapy on the part of the consultant astrologer for a number of reasons, the main one being that you can better understand the reality of psychological problems and how to deal with them if you know how it feels to sit in the client's chair. Having worked with your own particular issues you will approach someone else's with a greater degree of understanding and sensitivity. The role of the modern astrologer carries a greater measure of responsibility and requires a more professional attitude in keeping with the problems you are likely to encounter. Compared with this approach, the predictive fortune-telling brand of astrology is beginning to look distinctly dated.

Since no two charts and no two people are alike it is necessary for the astrologer to know where to pitch the reading. And the age of the person concerned is very important. Most people over 30 who have gone through their Saturn return tend to behave differently from those who haven't. Some people respond to imagery from mythology or fairy tales, some don't. Some understand psychological terminology, some want a more spiritual approach. Some know a bit about astrology, some know nothing at all.

For both astrologer and client the most mutually acceptable way of working seems to be a face-to-face taped consultation. If this idea doesn't appeal to you in the least, then you can request a written analysis. Many astrologers offer this service. Or if you are really only looking for a kind of broad-based character analysis, you can easily get a computer reading. However, neither of these more impersonal methods will enable you to ask questions. Often these arise naturally from the consultation itself. If you do want help with specific issues, if you want to understand why you keep finding yourself in the same situation, choose a taped consultation with a psychologically orientated astrologer.

Using astrology as a counselling tool is a way of identifying unhelpful patterns, connecting them to earlier experiences, and hopefully understanding why we have persisted in acting them out. An astrological reading will not change your life or your personality overnight, but it might discourage you from making the same old mistakes all over again. Instead of repeating this flawed pattern you could change the whole design. Use astrology in a practical way to throw some light on why you are no longer getting much out of your job or your relationship. It might give you the confidence to apply for that new job or train to be a homeopath or end the affair with your married lover or whatever goal it is you are aiming for.

WHERE CAN I FIND AN ASTROLOGER?

My first response to this question would be that news of good astrologers travels fast. People who have gained a lot from a chart reading will supply you with names and phone numbers. Word of mouth is a reliable guide. You can also get a list of qualified consultant astrologers from the main teaching body, the Faculty of Astrological Studies, which offers a thorough and professional astrological training. (Look in the appendix for the address of the Faculty and other teaching bodies.)

Many astrologers, both experienced and inexperienced, advertise in specialist publications. You might even find notices pinned up in natural healing centres. If in doubt, ask where they did their basic training. Staff in bookshops with a serious astrology section may also be able to point you in the right direction. Always make sure that you know how much the session will cost, where it will take place, how long it is likely to last, and whether you need to supply a tape. And do ask questions. I always let people know that I approach the chart from a psychological perspective so that they can decide at that point to make an appointment or not.

WHAT DOES AN ASTROLOGICAL READING INVOLVE?

No two astrologers will give exactly the same reading. I can only speak here about the work of those astrologers with which I am familiar. Most of them use the chart as a counselling tool. Some astrologers begin the chart with a general character reading and then move on to specific themes as shown by the chart. Others will begin the session by asking how they can help you and whether there is a specific area on which you would like to concentrate. You are free to comment and ask questions at any point. Astrologers actively encourage feedback. It is much more constructive for the astrologer to engage in a dialogue with you and hear your responses. The reading then becomes much more dynamic, and hopefully more satisfying for both parties. For astrologers, listening to sound of our own voices can be tiring, not to say boring. However, we do appreciate that not everyone finds it easy to talk about themselves. At the other end, of course, are those people who never stop talking. They don't seem to realise this until they play back the tape! A taped session can vary in length, but most astrologers allow an hour and a half to two hours.

WHAT SORT OF PEOPLE BECOME ASTROLOGERS?

According to a recent survey in *New Astrologer* (the magazine of the Faculty of Astrological Studies) significantly more women than men become consultant astrologers, the ratio being roughly two-thirds women to one-third men. Of those who filled in the questionnaire ages ranged from 30 to 70. Some work part-time from home, others full-time. Previous occupations range from teachers to management consultants. The article notes that 'today's consultant astrologers are basically astrological psychologists' and goes on to say that this approach 'gives the client the opportunity to actively take responsibility for his or her own life using the birth chart as a guide'.

SO YOU WANT TO BECOME AN ASTROLOGER

There are few training courses in natal astrology on offer outside London. The main teaching bodies are London based, but the Faculty of Astrological Studies organises good correspondence courses. A beginners course which teaches basic natal astrology, including how to draw up a birth chart, is offered by the Faculty of Astrological Studies, the Company of Astrologers and the Centre for Psychological Astrology (see appendix). The Faculty runs an advanced diploma course for those who have completed the beginners stage. The Centre for Psychological Astrology runs one-day seminars and an in-depth three-year professional training. A sound astrological knowledge is a necessary requirement for the Centre's three-year diploma course while members of the general public who are familiar with the basics will find the one-day seminars stimulating and valuable. In London the Astrological

Association and the Astrological Lodge hold meetings with guest speakers on Monday and Wednesday evenings respectively. If you want to find out more about groups in your region, contact the Astrological Association. The Urania Trust soon to open in London will have an excellent library, seminar rooms and bookshop as well as serving as an information centre for the astrological community (see appendix).

SOME LAST WORDS

Astrology has been around for a long time. Its fundamental principles are based on countless observations by millions of astrologers over the centuries. This ancient system stubbornly persists despite the technological complexity and sophistication of life in the twentieth century. Astrology has kept pace with modern technology as is evident, in one sense, from the wide range of astrological software on offer. Astrologers themselves have responded to their clients' increasingly sophisticated needs by offering a more professional service. At one end of the astrological spectrum, astrologers have penetrated the influential sphere of stock market analysis. At the other end, astrologers working with the birth chart are increasingly being asked for help with complex psychological problems.

Astrology cannot supply answers to problems on a global scale. What it can do is offer each of us, on an individual level, a practical tool for living. We can use the birth chart to identify patterns in our life experience. We have created these patterns ourselves, but some of them will not fit into our design in the way we intended. Then, it is up to us to improve it, working with what we've got, rather than what we haven't got. We can use the birth chart to work out a design which fits us better – one which can be better integrated into our overall pattern of development. An understanding of astrology can help us become attuned to the most productive ways of using the energies we have at our disposal. Then, we can consult the astrological clock to find out what time it is. It may be time for action, it may be time to watch and wait. Astrology is available now to help you to help yourself.

APPENDIX OF USEFUL ADDRESSES AND RESOURCES

NATIONAL ORGANISATIONS

Astrological Association
(Main Co-ordinating Body for Local Groups)
The Hon. Secretary
2 Waltham Close
Abbey Park
Nottingham NG2 6LE

Membership and Mail Order Service
P O Box 39
North P D O
Nottingham NG5 5PD

Astrological Lodge of London
BM Astrolodge
London WC1N 3XX

Meetings and lectures for the above organisations held at:
The Artworkers Guild
6 Queen Square
Bloomsbury
London WC1 3AR

Courses

Centre for Psychological Astrology
P O Box 890
London NW3 2JZ

Company of Astrologers
6 Queen Square
Bloomsbury
London WC1 3AR

Faculty of Astrological Studies
Registrar and Enquiry Office
(London Classes and Correspondence Course)
BCM Box 7470
London WC1N 3XX

Centres

Urania Trust (opening early 1989)
396 Caledonian Road
London N1 1DN

Computer Readings

Planet Word Processing
7 Soho Square
London W1V 5DP

SUGGESTED READING

Astrology

Liz Greene, *Astrology For Lovers*, Unwin Hyman, 1986
   Relating, Thorsons, 1987
Liz Greene with Howard Sasportas, *The Development of the Personality*, Routledge & Kegan Paul, 1987
Alice O. Howell, *Jungian Symbolism in Astrology*, Theosophical Publishing House, 1987
Eve Jackson, *Astrology, A Psychological Approach*, Dryad Press, 1987
Lindsay River and Sally Gillespie, *The Knot of Time*, Womens' Press, 1987
Howard Sasportas, *The Twelve Houses*, Thorsons, 1985

Science and Astrology

Dennis Elwell, *The Cosmic Loom*, Unwin Hyman, 1987

Psychology

Ean Begg, *Myth and Today's Consciousness*, Coventure, 1984
Irene Claremont de Castillejo, *Knowing Woman*, Harper & Row, 1974
Robin Skynner and John Cleese, *Families and How to Survive Them*, Methuen, 1983

Others

Lyall Watson, *Supernature*, Sceptre, 1986
   Dreams of Dragons, Sceptre, 1986

INDEX